G→A→M→I→F→Y

G→A→M→I→F→Y

HOW **GAMIFICATION** **MOTIVATES** PEOPLE TO DO **EXTRAORDINARY** THINGS

BRIAN BURKE

GARTNER, Inc.

First published by Bibliomotion, Inc.
39 Harvard Street
Brookline, MA 02445
Tel: 617-934-2427
www.bibliomotion.com

Printed in the United States of America

Library of Congress Cataloging-in-Publication Data

Burke, Brian, 1959–
    Gamify : how gamification motivates people to do extraordinary things / Brian Burke.
        pages cm
    Includes bibliographical references and index.
    ISBN 978-1-937134-85-3 (hardcover : alk. paper) — ISBN 978-1-937134-86-0 (ebook) — ISBN 978-1-937134-87-7 (enhanced ebook)
    1. Employee motivation. 2. Motivation (Psychology) 3. Games—Psychological aspects. 4. Organizational behavior. I. Title.
    HF5549.5.M63B875 2014
    658.3'14—dc23
                            2014000503

To Yolanda, for motivating me every day

CONTENTS

ACKNOWLEDGMENTS

Gamify is the product of a team effort over a few years, starting with Nick Gall's thought leadership on emergent systems and design thinking which formed an essential base to the development of many of the ideas in the book. My early research on gamification developed with collaboration from Mary Mesaglio, whose expertise on innovation management was essential, and Brian Blau, who provided invaluable insights into the world of game development.

Gartner's gamification research got a tremendous boost in 2011 with the support of the Gartner Fellows, in particular Tom Austin, Mark Raskino, Jackie Fenn, and Dave Aron, who provided the early support for developing the research topic under Gartner's Maverick Research Program. In 2012, David Willis and Betsy Burton were instrumental in supporting the development of a Gartner Special Report on gamification, with contributions from Rita Sallam, Jarod Greene, Cameron Haight, Chris Wilson, Elise Olding, Thomas Otter, Whit Andrews, Kevin Sterneckert, Steven Leigh, Don Scheibenreif, Simon Mingay, and Chet Geschickter which built out the research area.

Beyond research, *Gamify* was supported by a tremendous group of people including Andrew Spender, who sponsored the book at Gartner. While I have written research for many years, writing a book is quite a different project, and Heather Pemberton Levy from Gartner Books provided me with fantastic guidance and support in polishing the manuscript throughout its development. From the beginning, *Gamify* was a joint project with our publisher, Bibliomotion, and benefitted from the contributions of many people on the Bibliomotion team, particularly the founders, Erika Heilman and Jill Friedlander, who were reliable and supportive partners throughout the project.

Gamify would not have been possible without the support of my management team including Philip Allega, Anthony Bradley, and Peter Sondergaard, who helped to carve out the time and deflect the distractions which enabled me to write a book. Early reviewers included many of the aforementioned Gartner analysts, and also I'd like to thank Bernardo Crespo Velasco from BBVA, John Gehl from the Subway restaurant organization, and Nikola Ristivojevich from Ford Motor Company for their insightful reviews. The graphics in *Gamify* were improved tremendously thanks to the guidance and insights of Glenn Thode and Monica Virag.

My goal in Gamify was to ground the book in reality, highlight best practices in gamification and to leverage the knowledge of successful organizations. That was made possible with the collaboration of gamification practitioners from the many organizations that are highlighted in the book, including Cami Thompson, Clayton Nicholas, Cory Eisentraut, Craig Kielburger, David Cotterill, Dr. Jennifer Stinson, Imran Sayeed, Jill Schnarr, Naureen Meraj, Paul Wilmore, Rod Morris, Russell Bacon, Salman Khan, Stuart Thom, and Sven Gerjets.

Finally, but perhaps most importantly I thank my family, Yolanda, Geoff, and Shannon, who supported my disappearance for many hours of writing including countless lost evenings, weekends, and holidays. And the list would not be complete without my hound Gringo, who patiently listened to my ideas and kept me company in the middle of the night.

INTRODUCTION
Gamification: Beyond the Hype

In my basement, I keep a box of treasures that I have collected over a lifetime. In the box are things like my kindergarten report card and a collection of stones from all over the world. There's also a pin. It's not a fancy pin. It's just an old tin badge that has the original face removed and replaced by a piece of tape with "Norquay 51st—50,000 feet" written on it. It may not look like much but it means a lot to me. I've kept it for more than thirty years. Let me tell you how I got it.

In the late 1970s to early 1980s, I spent a couple of years as a ski bum working at Mt. Norquay in Banff National Park, Canada. The resort rewarded pins for skiing a certain number of vertical feet in a day. The fastest route was to start on the North American lift at the top of Norquay, cross under a stone bridge, and finish the last half on the legendary Lone Pine, a double black diamond. Skiing 25,000 feet earned you a bronze pin, 30,000 feet awarded you a silver pin, and 35,000 feet awarded you a gold pin. While I was there, the resort celebrated its fiftieth anniversary, and a new pin was added in commemoration. For skiing 50,000 vertical feet in a day, you could join the 50,000-foot club and receive a "platinum" pin. The catch was that Norquay only made fifty platinum pins available. To get the 50,000-foot pin required thirty-eight runs from the top. That meant nonstop skiing, all day long.

Like many of my coworkers at the resort, I earned the bronze, silver, and gold pins, and then kept an eye on the number of platinum pins left. Eventually, when only a few platinum badges remained, I decided it was time to go for it. The problem was that about ten other people also decided to try for the same badge that day. With only three platinum badges left, it turned into an all-day race.

During the course of the day, a couple of people dropped out of the competition and a few were forced out by injuries. One skier in front of me skidded through a corner at the midpoint and, realizing he wasn't going to make the tunnel in the stone bridge, flew off into the trees. I didn't stop.

By the end of the day, I had skied thirty-eight runs from the top, but I was fourth to finish. As the fifty-first skier to finish, I was just out of the running for a platinum pin. But my friends made a badge for me by tearing the face off an old button, sticking a piece of tape on it, and writing "50,000 feet." And that is how that old badge ended up in my treasure box. To me, it's priceless. I'm sure that you also have some treasured badges, ribbons, trophies, or other tokens of achievement. There's nothing new about motivating people with badges. They existed back in my ski bum days. Boy Scouts and Girl Scouts have been handing out badges for more than one hundred years. And military organizations have been awarding medals for centuries.

DIGITIZATION DRIVES SCALE

Handing out pins for achievements is not new—but the way that it is being done is transforming. When I went for the platinum pin at Norquay, the lift operators had a clipboard and put a tick mark on a piece of paper every time I got on the lift. The people I was competing with were all around me (mostly in front), and when my friends cheered me on, I could see and hear them. It was great, but the experience was limited to the physical world. Only a handful of skiers could take up the challenge on any given day, the other skiers and my friends were physically present, and it all happened in real time.

Fast-forward to today, and we see virtual badges popping up everywhere. They blur the physical and virtual worlds, and they scale to engage crowds of any size. Vail Resorts offers customers a gamified solution called EpicMix, which automatically tracks more than two hundred thousand skiers at ten resorts[1] and offers more than six hundred virtual pins as rewards. EpicMix users can race against friends or even against Olympic gold medalist Lindsey Vonn—without their competitors' physical presence nearby. With connections to Facebook, EpicMix users can share their pins, race medals, and photos with friends far away. Gamified solutions such as this leverage technology to break the barriers of scale, time, distance, connectedness, and cost.

But gamification is much more than virtual pins for skiers. Gamification engages and motivates people across all kinds of activities using game mechanics such as badges, points, levels, and leaderboards. What's new about gamification? Who is getting it right? How can your organization be successful with gamification? When should you think about using gamification in your organization? In this book, I will answer those questions and dig much deeper to explore the motivational power of gamification.

AN UNLIKELY JOURNEY

I'm not a gamer, nor a marketer, nor a behavioral scientist, nor a game designer. I'm an industry analyst in information technology with Gartner, Inc. With more than fourteen hundred analysts and consultants, Gartner provides technology insights to IT and business leaders in more than thirteen thousand organizations in eighty-five countries. What analysts do is identify trends, classify markets, and assess the impact of technologies and trends. We do that by finding the early adopters, analyzing the elements of success, establishing repeatable patterns, and projecting to the future. It's really about cutting away the hype and making sense of what is happening. For the past fifteen years, I've covered trends in enterprise architecture. And over the past several years, I've added gamification to my coverage.

People often ask me how I evolved from covering enterprise architecture to gamification—it seems like such a leap. But in fact, it's not a big jump. My research had been focused on using the constructs of games to engage people in innovation. Some organizations are serial innovators, and one of the characteristics they share is that innovation is largely decentralized, with many players encouraged to collaborate in teams and compete against other teams to innovate within a framework of goals and rules—just as in a game. I stumbled upon gamification in the course of developing research on innovation.

As I started to follow the trend, it quickly became clear that gamification is being applied to engage people in much more than innovation. It can also be used to develop skills and change behaviors. It improves lives. If this sounds like a hefty promise, read on. Over the past few years I have spoken with people in hundreds of organizations about gamification. What I found out is that gamification success is really all about motivating players to achieve their goals.

EARLY GAMIFICATION

Gamification is not just about applying technology to old engagement models, like awarding ski pins. Gamification creates entirely new engagement models, targeting new communities of people and motivating them to achieve goals they may not even know they have.

Have you ever "checked in" at a location? If so, you're probably familiar with Foursquare, an early and inspiring example of gamification. Launched at SXSW in 2009, Foursquare distinguished itself from other location-based services by awarding points for checking in to locations such as restaurants, theaters, and airports. A leaderboard offers an element of competition by showing users their scores ranked against their friends. Scores for what, you ask? Well, how about the "Bender" badge for checking in to bars four nights in a row? Or the "Gym Rat" badge for making ten check-ins at the gym in thirty days? "Mayorships" are awarded for checking in at a location more often than anyone else. Before Foursquare, who knew that people would want to be the mayor of their favorite hangouts? It didn't become a goal until Foursquare made it one.

Early users of Foursquare described it as addictive. Since launching in 2009, its user base has soared to forty million users.[2] Not only has Foursquare taken off, the gamification trend has skyrocketed along with it. Hundreds of gamified solutions have appeared over the past few years. Evangelists are singing gamification's praises, consultants are readying their services, technology providers are scrambling to add it to their offerings, and the press is buzzing. But with all of this attention comes the usual tendency to overhype. And what we see in the new technology business is that with hype comes inevitable failure, as organizations rush to implement a promising new solution without fully understanding the criteria for success. It's time to inject some reality into the conversation.

GAMIFICATION DEFINED

If you're bridling at this quirky term, *gamification*, let's do a short review of its history. The term reached the critical mass required to appear on Google Trends in the second half of 2010,[3] but the word has a longer history. Coined in 2002 by British consultant Nick Pelling, it was created as a "deliberately ugly word" to describe "applying game-like accelerated user interface design to make electronic transactions both enjoyable and fast."[4] In Pelling's view, gamification was all about hardware, and he created the term to describe the services of a start-up consultancy named Conundra Ltd. The term "gamification" outlived the consultancy, however, and has since come to describe something completely different.

While most people would agree that Pelling was successful in creating a truly ugly word, strangely, it stuck. Oxford Dictionaries selected "gamification" as a runner-up for the 2011 word of the year.[5] Many pundits would like to change the word, and some are even trying. Good luck! In my experience, once a term becomes part of the vernacular, it is impossible to replace, no matter how ugly it is.

While no broadly accepted definition of "gamification" exists, most definitions of the term share common characteristics. Gartner defines gamification as: *the use of game mechanics and experience design to digitally engage and motivate people to achieve their goals.* Let's pick this definition apart to gain a better understanding.

- *Game mechanics* describes the key elements that are common to many games, such as points, badges, and leaderboards.
- *Experience design* describes the journey players take with elements such as game play, play space, and story line.
- Gamification is a method to *digitally engage* rather than personally engage, meaning that players interact with computers, smartphones, wearable monitors, or other digital devices.
- The goal of gamification is to *motivate people* to change behaviors or develop skills, or to drive innovation.
- Gamification focuses on enabling players *to achieve their goals*—and as a consequence the organization achieves its goals.

BEYOND THE HYPE

Gamification has tremendous potential, but right now most companies aren't getting it right. The road to gamification success is full of pitfalls, and many companies don't understand how critical player motivation is to success. Widely publicized early successes have led some organizations to believe that gamification is a magic elixir for indoctrinating the masses and manipulating them to do the company's bidding. These organizations are mistaking people for puppets, and their transparently cynical efforts are doomed to fail. As a growing number of poorly designed gamified solutions appear, players will begin to suffer "badge fatigue" and actively avoid poorly designed solutions.

The truth is, gamification, like most emerging trends, is suffering from growing pains. In 2012, Gartner predicted that by 2014, 80 percent of current gamified applications will fail to meet business objectives, primarily due to poor design. This points to the number of bleeding-edge adopters that are getting it wrong. While that may sound like a dismal forecast for gamification, it is simply a stage that most emerging trends or technologies pass through. Since 1995, Gartner has used the Hype Cycle tool to track trends and technologies as they mature, and the path they take is both common and predictable.[6]

Gamification is one of more than nineteen hundred technologies and trends in almost one hundred different areas that Gartner tracks on the Hype Cycle. In the 2013 Hype Cycle for Emerging Technologies, Gartner placed gamification at the "peak of inflated expectations." But as we predicted in 2011, it is now heading into the "trough of disillusionment." Over the past three years, gamification has been hyped in the press, and current expectations exceed its potential. Recent inquiries with clients who misunderstand the potential of gamification include these examples:

Question: *We need to make the sales lead process more fun. The current process is that managers assign tasks to individual team members using a standard computer work-flow interface. It's really boring and managers are slow in assigning leads. We want to speed things up, so we are thinking of changing the interface so that the manager has a gun and the team members are the targets. The manager can then shoot the team members with the leads. What do you think?*

Answer: No, gamification is not about making activities look like a video game.

Question: *The long-term trend toward e-mail is slowly killing our postal services. We would like to use gamification to make sending real paper more fun and drive people to switch back to real mail rather than e-mail. How can we leverage gamification to convince customers to go back to sending more paper mail?*

Answer: If your product has no inherent advantages over the alternatives, I don't think gamification can help you.

Question: *We want to leverage gamification to coax the administrative staff to go above and beyond their duties by filling out expense reports for the salespeople. Currently, expense reporting is not part of their job, and we can't make it part of their job. We were wondering if we could use gamification to get them to do it.*

Answer: No, gamification is not going to help you get the administrative staff to do someone else's dirty work.

These clients had been oversold on what gamification is capable of achieving, and it's not surprising given the hype that currently surrounds it. Much of what is written on gamification today reinforces the perception that it can make anything fun. There are limits to what can be achieved with gamification, and the broader trend requires a course correction.

Right now, gamification is on a collision course with reality. If we continue down this path, as the failures pile up gamification may suffer a serious setback. We need to refocus on the realm of the possible. We need to focus on how gamification can be used by organizations to motivate people to achieve shared goals. My hope is that *Gamify* will change the current trajectory for gamification . . . just a little bit.

ACHIEVING GAMIFICATION SUCCESS

This book explores gamification as a means of motivating people to achieve their goals. It is not about rewards programs or video games, though we will explore how gamification is different from those things. Instead, *Gamify* guides business people on how to leverage gamification to empower their customers, employees, and communities to reach their goals. That's right: gamification is about motivating people to achieve *their own* goals, not the organization's goals.

That statement may seem counterintuitive to many business people. We are immersed in a culture that views business as hard-nosed, where the real masters are experts at separating people from their money. Of course, all businesses need to be profitable, but, as *Gamify* reveals, the personal goals of a company's customers, employees, and communities are often aligned with the organization's business goals. Like two sides of the same coin, shared goals may have different faces, but they are merely different views of the same thing. Later in the book, we will examine how organizations can provide goals that players will adopt as their own, and how those goals can become shared goals. If a business can identify the goals it shares with its audience or provide its audience with goals that are meaningful to them, and can leverage gamification to motivate these players to meet those goals, then the company will achieve the business outcomes it is looking for.

EARLY ADOPTERS

In most organizations, gamification got started in the marketing department but has since moved into many other areas of the business. Employee-facing solutions are the fastest-growing segment of the gamification market, and these internally focused solutions are set to take over customer- and community-facing solutions in the near future. Business leaders in marketing, customer loyalty, human resources, sales, product development, customer service, strategic planning, and innovation management are all using gamification to engage people and achieve business objectives.

Within information technology (IT) organizations, CIOs, CTOs, IT strategic planners, and enterprise architects need to understand gamification for three reasons. First of all, they need to know how to leverage gamification within the IT organization itself, particularly in the IT help desk, knowledge management, and social collaboration initiatives. Secondly, as gamification initiatives inevitably require applications to be developed and/ or supported, IT will be driving, or at least involved in, projects across the organization that target customers, employees, and communities of interest. Finally, IT managers need to be aware of gamification, as major vendors are starting to build game mechanics and analytics into many different software platforms and applications. This means that gamification is coming to your organization soon—whether you like it or not.

Organizations that are more aggressively adopting gamification already have multiple gamified solutions in place that support different business areas, address different target audiences, and achieve a wide range of business objectives. These organizations are starting to develop gamification centers of excellence to leverage the specialized skills required for these projects. These organizations are also considering how to integrate gamified solutions that touch the same target audience. For example, employees may be using one gamified solution for customer relationship management (CRM) and a different one for corporate training, and there are advantages in having an integrated view of each employee and how he interacts across different gamified solutions. This becomes even more critical when customers are using gamified solutions across multiple touch points. Increasingly, enterprise architects are being brought into these decisions, as they affect multiple business areas.

Given this wide variety of applications for gamification, people across the organization who are challenged to engage and motivate people should understand the opportunities to leverage gamification. In fact, in conversations with clients, we find that one of the early challenges gamification leaders face is determining which of the many opportunities to pursue first.

HOW THE BOOK IS ORGANIZED

Gamify takes you beyond the hype and explores the realistic potential for leveraging gamification. When applied effectively, gamification presents tremendous opportunity and can drive business results. After reading the following chapters, you will have an understanding of gamification, how it can be applied today, and how it is likely to evolve in the future. You will also understand the breadth of gamification's uses: (1) to achieve different objectives, (2) with different groups of people, and (3) in different industries, with many real-life examples. You won't find a lot of hype here; rather, this is a practical guide that will take you past the trough of disillusionment and onto the slope of enlightenment.

The book is divided into two parts. Part 1 introduces the concepts of gamification, describes how it can be used, and discusses when it is not appropriate. We'll look at examples of how gamification is being used to change behaviors, develop skills, and drive innovation with customers, employees, and communities of interest. Once you understand why and how, it's time to execute.

Part II takes you step-by-step through designing and launching a gamified solution, what's called the player experience design process. Design, in this case, entails a specific process for understanding your players and how to motivate them in the gamified experience. The player experience design process can be broken down into a number of steps that structure the tasks in a logical order, focus the design on achieving player goals, and reduce the time and risk to design a gamified solution.

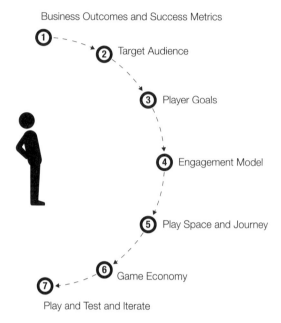

FIGURE I–1: The Player Experience Design Process

Gamify is intended for people who are interested in leveraging gamification in their organizations. While gamification offers tremendous opportunity, it is still early in the development of the trend and there are very few cookie-cutter implementations with proven successes that can easily be replicated. This book provides the guidance you need to move forward with a gamification initiative based on the lessons learned (good and bad) from many bleeding-edge adopters. But implementing a successful new gamified solution remains a challenge. You will likely be breaking new ground as you move forward with your first gamified solution. Welcome to the leading edge.

PART I

THE VALUE OF GAMIFICATION: ENGAGING THE CROWD

1

Motivation:
The Gamification Endgame

Every year the Hospital for Sick Children in Toronto, commonly known as SickKids, treats thousands of children who are battling cancer. As Canada's leading research hospital for children, the facility needs to gauge the effectiveness of various treatments so that it can use the best therapies while minimizing the pain for kids with cancer. Such information would also benefit kids with cancer around the world.

But first, the hospital needs daily reports from the children about their current levels of pain. Yet the kids are suffering. The treatments are painful, and patients are not always up to the task of filling out their pain journals, particularly on bad days. With inconsistent reporting, it's impossible for doctors to determine which treatments work best. What the hospital really needs is a way to inspire the kids to consistently provide critical information on their pain levels.

In previous studies, patients had often been inconsistent in filling out their journals, so researchers tried a different approach. They looked at the problem *from the kids' perspective* and decided to design an experience that engages the kids on a different level. Working with Cundari, a Toronto-based communications agency, the team created "Pain Squad," an iPhone app designed to collect daily information about children's pain levels. The Pain Squad app enlists kids as members of a special police force on a mission to hunt down pain. The app reminds children to report their pain levels twice a day. But simply moving the reporting from paper to an iPhone app wasn't enough. The app had to inspire the kids. The Pain Squad team needed to do more than just build an app; they needed to design an experience.

ENGAGING PLAYERS AT AN EMOTIONAL LEVEL

The challenge in getting children—or most people, for that matter—to do mundane or tedious tasks is to engage them at a deeper, more meaningful level. People find inspiration in many different ways. One way to motivate people is to present them with practical challenges, encourage them as they progress through levels, and get them emotionally engaged to achieve their very best. Gamification does just that. At its core, gamification is about engaging people on an emotional level and motivating them to achieve their goals.

Engagement gets a lot of airtime. Marketers focus on customer engagement, employers focus on employee engagement, educators focus on student engagement—and the list goes on. But the focus on engagement is often on the quantity of interactions rather than the quality—and these are two completely different things. Not all engagement is equal.

For example, dozens of research papers on employee engagement demonstrate the correlation between high levels of engagement and increased productivity, profits, retention, and quality, among other benefits.[1] But the majority of American workers are not engaged or, worse, they are actively disengaged.[2] Recent research indicates that engagement is not one-dimensional, and it is important to distinguish between *emotional engagement* and *transactional engagement*. According to the Chartered Institute of Personnel and Development (CIPD), transactional engagement is "shaped by employees' concern to earn a living and to meet minimal expectations of the employer and their coworkers," while emotional engagement is "driven by a desire on the part of employees to do more for the organization than is normally expected and in return they receive more in terms of a greater and more fulfilling psychological contract."[3]

The distinction between emotional engagement and transactional engagement is visible far beyond employee/organizational relationships. Every interaction is a balance, with some weighing more on the emotional side and others being more transactional. If you are trying to lose a few pounds and are going to the gym to work out, think about how you engage in that activity. Some of the engagement may be transactional—you need to spend twenty minutes on the treadmill. But when you step on the scale and see that you've lost five pounds, there is an emotional engagement. You can see progress toward your goal, and you know you need to focus on the goal, not on the treadmill. Clearly, these engagement dimensions are not mutually exclusive but rather combinatorial. The problem is that organizations often rely primarily on transactional engagement strategies in their interactions. We need to shift our focus to emotional engagement if we want to truly motivate people.

NOT ALL REWARDS ARE EQUAL

When SickKids hospital developed its Pain Squad app, it had to address the types of rewards the app would give the children. While many parents and educators are familiar with rewarding kids for good work with stickers, cookies, or allowance money, they know well the limitations of simple rewards when it comes to real behavior change. According to Dr. Jennifer Stinson, who led the study at SickKids, "Previous similar diary-type studies typically incentivize the patients to complete their diaries by paying them. In this study, we wanted to get away from paying the kids, and in working with Cundari, we decided to use gamification to motivate the kids."[4]

The Pain Squad mobile app creates an experience for the children in which they are playing the role of a police officer in a special force. The app includes a progression structure, so that when the children complete their pain report three days in a row, they progress from rookie to sergeant and through ranks until they finally become a chief. Like leveling up in a video game, movement up the ranks in the squad is visible to the kids. At Pain Squad Headquarters, the kids can see the badges they have earned and when they need to fill out their next report. To add even more inspiration, the team recruited some of the heroes from Canada's leading police television shows. The casts from *Flashpoint* and *Rookie Blue* collaborated to create a series of videos to encourage the children to complete their reports, and these are sprinkled liberally throughout the Pain Squad mission.

According to Stuart Thom, interactive designer/developer at Cundari, "The actors appear to be actually speaking to you because they are addressing you by your rank."[5] The app gives the kids a sense of control when it comes to managing their pain. According to the mother of one of the kids, "It makes her feel that she's a part of this."[6] Instead of paying kids to provide information that the researchers need, Pain Squad engages them in an inspiring mission. Most importantly, they are contributing to something bigger than themselves.

GAMIFICATION IS ALL ABOUT MOTIVATION

What the SickKids staff was learning is that extrinsic and intrinsic rewards provide starkly different outcomes. In his book *Drive: The Surprising Truth About What Motivates Us*, Daniel Pink examined the science of motivation and how extrinsic and intrinsic rewards affect behavior. In it, he cited numerous studies showing that extrinsic rewards are not sufficient to sustain engagement, and sometimes have the opposite effect. Extrinsic rewards "can deliver a short-term boost—just as a jolt of caffeine can keep you cranking a few more hours. But the effect wears off—and worse, can reduce a person's long-term motivation."[7] Pink concludes that intrinsic motivators have three essential elements: "(1) Autonomy—the desire to direct our own lives; (2) Mastery—the urge to make progress and get better at something that matters; and (3) Purpose—the yearning to do what we do in service of something larger than ourselves."

Gamification uses primarily intrinsic rather than extrinsic rewards. As we will see a little later, the distinction between intrinsic and extrinsic rewards is one of the ways we can distinguish gamification from rewards programs. Intrinsic rewards sustain engagement because they engage people at an emotional level. Extrinsic rewards can certainly be used to motivate people, but the motivation occurs at a transactional level.

The series of MasterCard "Priceless" commercials captured the difference between emotional and transactional experiences succinctly with the slogan, "There are some things money can't buy. For everything else there's MasterCard."[8] Engagement can be bought, at least for the short term, with extrinsic rewards, but for emotional engagement you need to focus on intrinsic rewards.

Now let's examine the three elements of motivation (autonomy, mastery, and purpose) through the lens of gamification.

Autonomy—the desire to direct our own lives. In effective gamified solutions, players opt in to participate, and once they do, they make choices about how they will proceed through the challenges to achieve their goals. Players are given the opportunity to discover and learn using different paths through the solution. In some gamified solutions there are no paths at all. Players are given goals, tools, rules, and a space to "play" without being directed on the next steps to take.

Mastery—the urge to make progress and get better at something that matters. We all have a deep-seated need to improve in aspects of our lives, but often we lack the motivation to take the first step. Gamification provides the positive feedback and easy on-boarding that can motivate people to start performing better in a chosen area. But mastery is not an attainable goal, it is a journey. There are many signposts along the way that indicate progress, but there is never an end point. In virtually all of life's pursuits—whether it is running, painting, or learning a language—there is always another level. Gamification is about getting better at something.

Purpose—the yearning to act in service of something larger than ourselves. By definition, gamified solutions are distinguished from traditional games by their purpose. Gamification is focused on one or more of three objectives: changing behaviors, developing skills, or driving innovation. Gamification must start and finish with a purpose that is centered on achieving meaningful player goals. As we saw with the Pain Squad app, the kids played a critical role in the effort to reduce pain for cancer patients. It's a goal much larger than themselves.

Cundari realized how important it was to create an environment of intrinsic rewards to motivate the children to complete their pain journals. As Cory Eisentraut, group creative director at Cundari, put it:

> This app actually became very empowering for the kids. We didn't realize at the time we started developing this app how little control the kids have over their lives. Nothing in their lives is up to them. They are constantly being told when to go to appointments, what surgeries they're going to have, and how long they will be in hospital. None of that gets decided by them. So much

is taken away from them. They get pulled out of school. They have to say goodbye to their friends for long periods of time.

What this app actually became was their control—a tool that gave them some power over their disease. The value exchange was more than being about fun, it was about actually being a part of the cure, being a part of their treatment. In a very real way, the data that they were giving the doctors was not only going to help them, but it was going to help future patients. We weren't sure if the kids were really going to get that, but they absolutely did.

DON'T MISTAKE BUSINESS GOALS FOR PLAYER GOALS

Often, we fail to achieve our goals not because the goal is uninspiring but because the path to achieving the goal is too hard, takes too long, or we don't know where to start. The goal is not the problem; it is the path to achieving the goal that is the problem. Outlining that path is one way that gamification can help. By breaking a goal into a series of manageable steps and encouraging people along the way, gamified solutions can help them achieve their goals.

One of the key problems in many gamified solutions is that they are focused on getting players to achieve the organization's goals rather than players' goals. Gamified solutions must put players' motivations and goals first and make them the primary design objective. This player-centric design approach is not intuitive, but every design decision must be focused on motivating players and enabling them to be successful in achieving their goals. First, though, designers need to understand players' needs and ambitions. The solution must build a series of challenges that engages the players at an emotional level and motivates them to achieve a goal that is meaningful to them.

Pain Squad achieved this synergy and has been a tremendous success. According to Dr. Stinson:

> In a previous study for kids with arthritis we had a 76 percent compliance rate over a two- to three-week period. And compliance definitely dropped off in the second and third week, I think because of the lack of motivation. That study used an electronic diary, but it didn't have the motivation of Pain Squad. Using the Pain Squad app, we did a feasibility study with about twenty-two kids where we had them use it twice a day over a two-week period. We had almost 90 percent compliance, and it did not differ between week one and week two, nor between boys and girls. I think it was because of gamification. They really wanted to move up the ranks by the end of the two-week period.

Of course, the organizational objectives must also be met. It would be unrealistic to expect an organization to spend time, talent, and treasure without a return on investment. Player-centric design does not negate the organization's goals, but supplants them with the player's goals as the primary objective. The organization's goals are a by-product. If the player's goals are aligned with the organization's goals, then the organizational goals will be achieved as a consequence of the player achieving her goals. The positive results of the Pain Squad implementation are clear. The kids feel like they are contributing to something larger than themselves and they gain some control over their lives. The researchers, in turn, get the data they need. It's clearly a win–win.

Sometimes players must be provided goals to adopt as their own. As we saw with Foursquare, the goal of becoming "mayor" of a location was not one that came to people naturally, rather it was provided to players and they adopted it as their own. Often, achievements are only meaningful to a specific community, and experience designers will need to create awards that will motivate the target audience. For example, a "firestarter badge" is not something a young boy knows that he wants until he becomes a Cub Scout. Within that community, the badge is meaningful. As we go through many of the examples later in the book, you will find that the motivation to reach goals is often created through the community, where social norming motivates people to achieve goals that are valued within the player community. Simply stated, motivation to achieve is often fabricated by experience designers and adopted by the target audience.

Depending on the application, it may be possible for the organization to provide goals that players will adopt. But there may be cases where player goals and organizational goals are simply not aligned, nor can they be aligned. In these cases, gamification may not be the right approach, and offering to pay participants or providing some other tangible reward may be the only answer.

But not all organizations understand this fine distinction between extrinsic and intrinsic rewards or how to engage players to reach their goals. Many still view gamification as a glorified loyalty program. Or they see gamification as a way of turning some unpleasant task into a game. In the next chapter, we'll look a little further at what makes gamification different from rewards programs and video games.

WRAP UP

- ✓ Gamification engages people at an emotional level, which is far more powerful than typical transactional engagement strategies.
- ✓ Intrinsic rewards can sustain engagement, whereas extrinsic rewards have a less durable impact and may even serve to discourage players.

✓ People are motivated by maintaining a sense of autonomy, progressing toward mastery, and engaging with a purpose larger than themselves.

✓ Player-centric design starts with an understanding of the players' goals and ambitions and strives for an experience that engages players at an emotional level to help them achieve a goal that is meaningful to them.

✓ Gamification breaks larger goals into smaller practical challenges, encouraging players as they progress through levels, and engages them emotionally to achieve their very best.

✓ If the player's goals are aligned with the organization's goals, then the organizational goals will be realized as a consequence of the player achieving her goals.

2

Give Meaning to Players

Now that we understand what gamification is, we also need to understand what it is not. There is a lot of confusion and debate surrounding the similarities and differences between video games, rewards programs, and gamification. Because they share some similar constructs, such as points and levels, people often think they are the same and that the principles that are applied to one can be applied to another. But video games and rewards programs are very different from gamification, and it's important to have a clear understanding of those differences to avoid confusion.

Companies that provide rewards and incentive programs see themselves as having "done gamification for a long time," and find it difficult to distinguish gamification from rewards programs. However, the primary motivators used in these different approaches push different buttons. Loyalty, rewards, and incentive programs function as a payback for players who complete certain actions prescribed by the sponsor organization. This is not to say that gamification is somehow superior, but it is best to know which buttons you are trying to push when targeting people's engagement.

Some of the best-known rewards systems are airline programs. While most of the rewards in these programs would be considered tangible (for example, free flights or VIP lounge access), they also include some intangible rewards such as priority check-in and boarding. The distinction between tangible and intangible rewards in airline programs was central to the story of *Up in the Air*. In the film, George Clooney plays Ryan Bingham, a business consultant who specializes in firing people from organizations that are downsizing. He spends most of his time either flying or in hotels, and his life is as empty as his apartment—he has no spouse, no real friends, and little contact with his family. His passion is collecting frequent-flyer points and his goal is to collect ten million miles and join an exclusive group of just six people who have done it. This group is so exclusive that "More people have walked on the moon." The reward for achieving this goal is, "You get lifetime executive status, you get to meet the chief pilot, Maynard Finch...and they put your name on the side of a plane."[1] Interestingly, the rewards that Ryan values most are those that have an emotional attachment for him, not the free flights.

We could conclude that Ryan Bingham is emotionally engaged with his frequent flyer program, but I would posit that he is the exception. As a frequent-flyer myself (though not quite at Bingham's level), I can attest that I am not emotionally attached to rewards programs. Rewards programs use some of the same game mechanics (points, levels) as gamified solutions, but they mostly engage people on a transactional level. They are essentially a payback scheme: "Take ten flights and get one free." While these programs have proven their value over time, this type of offer doesn't reach most people on an emotional level. Loyalty programs don't inspire people. They rely on a transactional engagement that appeals to people's logic rather than their emotions.

WHAT IS DIFFERENT ABOUT GAMIFICATION?

It's not surprising that people collect points to take advantage of a free flight—in fact, it's illogical to leave money on the table. The primary distinction between gamification and traditional

incentive and rewards programs is that gamification engages
people in a way that is meaningful to them. Understanding this
distinction can help organizations focus on what makes gamification such a powerful technique to engage a target audience.

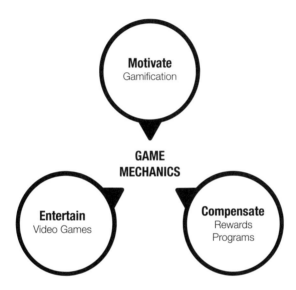

FIGURE 2–1: Gamification, Video Games, and Rewards Programs

Gamification, video games, and rewards programs are similar in a few ways:

- They engage "players" voluntarily.
- They use game mechanics such as points and levels.
- They are interactive.
- They incorporate progression to move players to the next
  level.

But the differences are more important than the similarities. Video games, rewards programs, and gamification engage
people on very different levels and they have entirely different
purposes.

- **Games** primarily engage players on a whimsical level to **entertain them.**
- **Rewards programs** primarily engage players on a transactional level to **compensate them.**
- **Gamification** engages players on an emotional level to **motivate them.**

Games have only one mission: to entertain the players. To achieve that, video games use elaborate story lines, graphics, and animation to create realistic experiences for players. The goal is to get players immersed in the game world and the role that they play in the game.

Rewards programs focus on developing higher value and repeated transactions with customers or on rewarding employees for achieving goals. The most common of these are airline, hotel, and retailer loyalty programs, but they also include employee incentive programs and other categories as well.

This doesn't necessarily mean that there are hard lines between video games, gamification, and rewards programs. As we will see a little later, rewards programs do provide some incentives that engage people at an emotional level. Some gamification solutions have tangible rewards in the mix of incentives. Serious games are games with a purpose, and they have been around for decades. This category of games mixes entertaining video game elements with educational material to make learning more fun. The distinction is really the *primary* engagement model, incentive structure, and purpose.

To understand and distinguish the primary purpose of gamification from video games and rewards programs, it is useful to follow the money. Video games, gamification, and rewards programs all cost money. Someone provides it, someone is playing it, and one of those two is paying for it. There is a value exchange. In video games, the player pays the video game developer for the entertainment value of the game. In rewards and incentive programs, the sponsor organization (airline, hotel, retailer, or employer) pays the player with tangible rewards for the value of repeat business (with customers) or increased productivity (with employees). In gamification, the sponsor organization and the players have overlapping goals. Typically, the sponsor organization pays for the gamified solution and the players play for free. Because the goals are shared, the value is also shared between the players and the sponsor organization, and there is no flow of money or tangible rewards between the player and the sponsor organization.

As we have seen, video games, gamification, and rewards programs have different purposes, engage people at different levels, and have different value exchanges. But because they all use game mechanics such as points, levels, and leaderboards, these shared characteristics have led people to conflate the three, and this confusion is the cause of many noisy debates.

GAMIFICATION IS NOT ABOUT FUN

While it seems counterintuitive, gamification is not about fun. Upon hearing the term *gamification*, many people jump to the conclusion that we can make activities fun by adding points and badges, just like a game. There are countless websites, blogs, and news articles, including some of our early research that improbably claim that "gamification can make work fun." The community of video game developers generally dislikes gamification, as it "cheapens" the work they do, which is understandable. Some people argue that video games are a form of art with creative elements such as graphics, music, and storytelling. In contrast, gamification is centered more on the science of motivation. Some are quite passionate in their disapproval. According to Ian Bogost, professor at Georgia Tech and founding partner of Persuasive Games, "Gamification is marketing bullshit, invented by consultants as a means to capture the wild, coveted beast that is videogames and to domesticate it for use in the grey, hopeless wasteland of big business, where bullshit already reigns anyway."[2]

Jesse Schell is a professor of entertainment technology at Carnegie Mellon University and the founder of Schell Games. In his 2013 D.I.C.E. Summit keynote speech he said, "Adding game mechanics to things that aren't games is really hard."[3] He compares gamification to chocolate coatings on things that are not sweets, like cottage cheese and staplers. While chocolate makes some things better, the effect is not universal. He jokingly calls adding chocolate to everything "chocification."

Given the fact that many of the aficionados of gamification also understand and promote it as a way of turning nongame activities into games, it's not surprising the video game community is upset. While both video games and gamification use game mechanics such as points, badges and leaderboards, games and gamification are fundamentally different. Now that we understand the differences between gamification and games, let's examine how rewards programs differ from gamification.

GAMIFICATION IS NOT A PAYBACK

Rewards programs typically provide members with discounts and offers such as free flights or hotel stays for repeat business. While they are often called "loyalty programs," perhaps a more appropriate name would be "kickback scheme," especially if the intent is to influence the buying behaviors of people traveling on corporate expense accounts with personally redeemable rewards. Remember Ryan Bingham?

The same is true of most employee incentive programs. Employees are given tangible rewards in return for some specific result, perhaps a trip to Hawaii for achieving a sales target or tickets to a football game for meeting a production goal. In these cases, employees are rewarded for achieving organizational goals with scant regard to whether the employee shares the goal. It's not necessary for the employee to share the organizational goal. The employees have a different goal: winning the prize.

IS GAMIFICATION NEW?

Craig Kielburger, angered by the injustice of child labor, became a social activist at the age of twelve. After traveling from his home in Canada to South Asia to speak to child laborers, he and his brother, Marc, founded what became Free The Children, an international charity and youth movement with the goal to "empower and enable youth to be agents of change." Free the Children designed its Adopt a Village approach to enable sustainable change in communities by focusing on education, clean water and sanitation, health, alternative income and livelihood, and agriculture and food security. The program operates in communities in Kenya, India, Ecuador, Nicaragua, rural China, Haiti, Sierra Leone, and Ghana.[4]

In addition, Craig is passionate about inspiring young people to act for global change. As he told me, "So often, young people think they are alone. When we see the problems in our schools, and in our world, they are so overwhelming. It can make us feel so insignificant." So Free The Children created We Day, a series of events designed to inspire youth to act.[5]

We Day events, held in nine cities in Canada and three in the United States, bring together tens of thousands of youths in a stadium for a day of education, engagement, and inspiring speeches and performance centered around critical local and global issues. Participants must earn tickets to attend through service that has a positive social impact both locally and globally. Attendees leave the event feeling connected to a community of like-minded youth who are excited to make a difference in the world.

The question is how to sustain that engagement and motivation throughout the year and reach an even broader audience. As Craig explained, "Now the challenge, of course, is that We Day is one day. Our dream is to take that spirit and feeling of connectivity and empowerment and education that we see at We Day, and make it something that is far more constant in your life, and far more empowering—because you can connect on a daily basis with that energy and live that same spirit 365 days a year."

To answer this challenge, Free The Children partnered with Canadian telecommunications company TELUS to introduce We365, a gamified solution to digitally engage and motivate youth throughout the year. We365 targets youth who are committed to social good and extends the motivation of We Day to enable people to support causes, complete challenges, track and verify volunteer hours, and be part of a larger community of people who are taking action for social good. Jill Schnarr, vice president of community affairs at TELUS, told me, "Success is really inspiring a much wider group of kids, beyond We Day, both nationally and internationally, to feel like they have the tools to be able to give back, and to see them acting in whatever causes they are most passionate about so that real, true social change is happening."

As we can see from the Free The Children example, what's new about gamification is that it uses digital engagement to extend motivation beyond the limits of the physical world. There are numerous advantages of using a digital model:

Scale—digital interactions can connect to audiences of any size

Time—digital interactions are not dependent on other people being available in real time

Distance—thanks to the Internet, digital interactions are available anywhere

Connectedness—with social networking, your friends are always nearby

Cost—digital interactions scale at a much lower cost than face-to-face models

Craig recognizes the power of using the digital engagement model to extend the inspiration of We Day to make participating in social change a year-round activity, and even beyond youth to include adults and corporations. He says, "I think the day will come in the near future where We365 eclipses We Day. It will be far bigger in terms of the frequency of use and the brand recognition and in the empowering experience."

ENABLING TRENDS

As we will see, gamification and digital engagement are extending motivation in many different areas. There are several adjacent trends that are also driving the adoption of gamification:

Disintermediation. Elimination of the middleman has been an inevitable result of direct access to products and services. We have already experienced the impact of disintermediation with travel agents, insurance brokers, stockbrokers, and booksellers. Disintermediation is extending to other areas as well, including coaching and training. Increasingly, the people delivering these services are being replaced by cheap or free services that are available on the Internet or via smartphone apps. Gamification provides a form of motivation in which personal contact has been replaced with a digital engagement model.

Social networking. These days, people don't need to leave their homes to connect with friends or even to meet new people. This type of social connection is having an impact on traditional motivation approaches that rely on face-to-face meetings. For example, a big part of the success of Weight Watchers can be attributed to the social interactions that are fostered through meetings. With social networking sites like Facebook, getting support from a group of people who are going through the same change is inexpensive and easy. Gamification leverages social media to increase the power of social circles, allowing users to enlist encouragement from friends and amplifying the value of achievements.

The wisdom of the crowd. Over the past decade or so, organizations have shifted from sourcing innovation from a small group of people to broadly embracing the crowd. The Internet has made it possible to engage large groups of people to develop new ideas. The crowd is already connected, and the collective wisdom is ready to tap; gamification engages and motivates crowds to participate in innovation.

These adjacent trends are replacing human interactions with digital interfaces and allowing people to have access to vast resources through the Internet, to be connected to everybody, and to provide built-in support groups. What's missing is the motivation, and that's where gamification comes in. In some cases, digitally delivered motivation displaces some forms of engagement and motivation that were traditionally delivered in a face-to-face model. For example, using a face-to-face model, Weight Watchers leverages the same types of motivational tools that gamification uses, and now the company is beginning to feel the threat of digital engagement. Weight Watchers reported a decline in second-quarter 2013 revenues "resulting from lower revenues in the meetings business as it experienced weaker volumes globally."[6] It also experienced declines in customers. "What we've seen is a deteriorating trend in recruitments, particularly on our online business and we feel that some of that is driven by the continued sudden explosion of interest in free apps and activity monitors," said chief financial officer Nicholas Hotchkin.[7] The market responded with a 19 percent decline in share price and the CEO resigned.

LEVERAGING GAMIFICATION TO ENGAGE THE CROWD

When it comes to gamification, "the more the merrier" certainly applies. Gamification provides leverage and is best applied when the target audience is large. The concept of leverage works in a couple of ways: (1) a single solution can be used to engage a virtually limitless number of players; and (2) the larger and more diverse the crowd, the more likely people are to find innovative solutions to problems. Additionally, gamification is implemented as a digital solution with little or no direct human interaction from the solution-provider side. The players are playing against one another and/or the game itself. Gamified solutions provide high leverage, as they are deployed once and used by many.

Gamified solution costs per user can be very high if the number of users is small. As with any solution, the design and development costs are fixed and the deployment costs are variable. Because the design and development costs will be incurred regardless of the audience size, deploying to a larger crowd is less costly on a per-user basis.

Conversely, if the audience is small, a direct personal engagement model may be more appropriate (and less costly) than a gamified solution. Simply stated, if the target audience is a group of ten people who are all runners in training, it is better to personally coach them than it is to build a solution that simulates coaching. Gamification is often a proxy for human encouragement and interaction. With smaller groups, real human interaction is likely to work better and cost less.

Audiences for gamified solutions typically break into three segments: employees, customers, and communities of interest. While it may be necessary to narrow the target audience even further, generally speaking it is a good idea to cast a wide net. This is particularly important for gamified solutions that crowd-source innovative ideas, because a larger pool is likely to include people with different perspectives and experiences.

Employee focus. Certain types of gamified solutions are typically deployed within organizations to engage and motivate either the entire employee base (as we will see in innovation games) or a subset of the employee base with a specific goal, such as on-boarding new hires or improving performance for employees within a specific business function like the service desk or sales.

Customer focus. Organizations deploy customer-focused solutions to add value to a product offering, to train customers on product use, to enlist customers to cocreate new products, and for many additional purposes. Defining the customer is always a challenge, but the opportunity in customer-focused solutions is to engage consumers of products and services.

Community-of-interest focus. Gamified solutions for this group are often openly available on the Internet to anyone who wants to use them. The players in these games are self-selecting and they opt in based on their interests. Gamification can be used to motivate ecologically minded consumers to recycle, to help those interested develop new language skills, or even to engage citizen scientists in solving complex scientific challenges. There are as many communities of interest as there are areas of interest.

	Customers	Employees	Community
Change Behaviors	Nike	DIRECTV	AHA
Develop Skills	Change Healthcare	NTT Data	Khan Academy
Drive Innovation	Barclaycard	DWP	Quirky

FIGURE 2–2: Target Audiences and Uses of Gamification

In addition to the three target audiences—customers, employees, and communities of interest—gamification is employed for three categories of use: changing behaviors, developing skills, and driving innovation. Figure 2–2 serves two purposes: (1) the axes describe the audiences and uses for a gamified application; and (2) the organizations listed provide examples that we will see later in the book of gamification solutions that address each of these uses and audiences. If you can't locate the target audience and the use on this chart, review the earlier sections in this chapter to determine whether gamification is the appropriate approach for your goal.

In the remaining chapters of part 1, we will explore how the organizations in the chart and others have used gamification to change behavior, develop skills, and drive innovation across each type of audience. Regardless of the audience you are engaging, the steps are often similar within each use area. In the next few chapters, we will also examine some common pathways to success for each of these uses.

WRAP UP

✓ Gamification, games, and rewards programs all use game mechanics such as points, badges, and leaderboards, but the similarities end there.

✓ Loyalty, rewards, and incentive programs function as a pay-back for players who complete certain actions prescribed by the sponsor organization. The sponsor organization bears the costs of the program and of the rewards to players.

✓ Games have no purpose other than entertaining the players. When a game is successful, players pay for the cost of the game plus the profit to the provider.

✓ Gamification is about motivating players to achieve goals that are shared by the provider and the player. Normally, the provider pays for the solution and the players participate for free.

✓ What's new about gamification is that it uses a digital model to extend engagement and motivation beyond face-to-face interactions, breaking the barriers of scale, time, distance, connectedness, and cost.

✓ Disintermediation, social networking, and crowdsourcing are adjacent trends that enable gamification.

✓ Gamification serves three primary purposes: changing behaviors, developing skills, and driving innovation for three target audiences: customers, employees, and communities of interest.

3

Changing Behavior One Step at a Time

We are creatures of habit. Think about your morning routine. If you are like most people, you operate on autopilot. Routines make life easy. They form over time to become an automatic response to seeking pleasure and avoiding pain. But what if you want to change some part of that routine? You may have a desire to develop a good habit or overcome a bad habit. In either case, the change is hard. For most people, a little motivation can make all the difference. Sometimes, we need help and guidance from experts to make the change, and other times we just need a little nudge. Gamification can provide both.

MOTIVATING ATHLETES

Geoffrey deployed to Iraq in 2008, and when he returned to the United States, he faced many stresses in his life. He was divorced and his children were living on the other side of the country, fifteen hundred miles away. As Geoffrey told me, "I had idle hands, and we know what happens when you have idle hands. I began to eat to deal with the stress until I reached 270 pounds. Then I had a wake-up call."[1]

Geoffrey knew he needed to lose weight. He had read that Nike was revolutionizing fitness with Nike+, so he decided to get some Nike+ shoes with the iPod sensor. He found the experience transformative. As Geoffrey recalls:

Being an absolute geek and completely into technology, I tried them out. My first run was only .86 miles and I couldn't breathe by the time I decided to stop. After that, every run got easier. Every run got longer. Before I knew it, I lost sixty pounds. The thing is that I couldn't stop. In the first year I accumulated 370 miles. I couldn't stop there. Here I am, almost four years later, and I'm on the cusp of hitting a thousand miles. I gained a little bit of the weight back. I'm currently at 240 pounds. But I'm healthier and happier than I ever was at any point in my life.

Geoffrey is just one of the more than eleven million Nike+ users. Since first launching the Nike+ iPod Sport Kit in 2006, Nike has launched a suite of products designed to motivate athletes to achieve their goals. The Nike+ product line has expanded to include an iPhone app to track running, basketball shoes with sensors that track movements, and the Nike+ Kinect Training application to aid working out at home, just to name a few. Nike's mission is "To bring innovation and inspiration to every athlete in the world. If you have a body, you are an athlete."[2]

With the introduction of the FuelBand, Nike is bringing innovation and inspiration to an even broader audience of athletes. The FuelBand records movement using an accelerometer and calculates the value for different types of movement into NikeFuel points, making NikeFuel a common currency for movement and allowing comparisons across different types of activities. The clever thing about the FuelBand is that the accelerometer can recognize different movement patterns like jogging, walking up the stairs, or strolling on the street. Working with Arizona State University, Nike created baseline values for the oxygen uptake for each of these recognized movement patterns, and these were recorded in a lab. The FuelBand then applies a factor for each movement type to determine the NikeFuel points earned for each activity. This was an important objective for Nike, because the company wants to reach all athletes. As Stefan Olander, Nike's VP of digital sport, states, "The more people move, the better it is. So, we have products that can inspire and enable everyone to be more active."[3]

It seems to be working. In the first year after the launch, Nike+ FuelBand users racked up 409 billion NikeFuel points, which is the equivalent of running forty-four million marathons. The energy used is enough to power 6,772 houses.[4] That's a lot of motivation!

REWRITING THE CUSTOMER ENGAGEMENT MODEL

Nike's digital sport division has built a business around engaging and motivating athletes to achieve their goals, and gamification is an integral part of the products it delivers in this space. Nike+ is a leading-edge example of building gamification into the core product offering, but Nike is not alone. Many organizations use gamification to change customer behaviors in a variety of innovative ways.

Reducing environmental impact is good for consumers, companies, and the planet. Opower works with energy companies and uses behavioral science to motivate people to reduce energy consumption. It designs a choice architecture for consumers, so they are motivated to use less energy. For example, Opower invokes social norms by providing data to homeowners that compares their energy consumption to that of their neighbors. Social norms are expectations for how we should behave in a group. If you are using more energy than your neighbors, you will naturally feel you are deviating from accepted group behaviors; most people want to align their behaviors with group social norms.

Opower uses a variety of tools from behavioral science such as triggers and autonomy to motivate people to reduce energy consumption. Triggers are a call to action. They can be simple reminders that provide guidance on how to change a behavior. Presenting energy- efficient behavior as a choice provides people with the autonomy to opt-in to becoming more energy efficient. The success of the business depends on it. According to Rod Morris, SVP of marketing and operations, "The entire premise of our business relates to changing behavior. If we don't change people's behavior, we don't get paid."[5] Working with utilities, Opower reaches twenty-two million homes and has motivated people to reduce three terawatt hours of energy use.[6] To give you some idea of scale, that's enough energy to power St. Louis and Salt Lake City combined.

Building gamification incentives that move beyond tangible rewards requires different thinking about what the customer values. Often, customers place a high value on rewards based on self-esteem or social recognition. As I mentioned earlier, EpicMix enables skiers and snowboarders at Vail Resorts to track vertical feet, and rewards accomplishments with pins. It also has a leaderboard that allows competition among friends, family, and even professional skiers.

As we have learned, social recognition is a powerful motivator. According to Darren Jacoby, director of customer relationship marketing at Vail Resorts, "You know, part of skiing is bragging. So this gives our guests the ability to brag and compete with their friends."[7] From a business model perspective, Vail Resorts leverages gamification to make skiing a more engaging experience and enhances the value of the product it offers to customers. In the 2010–2011 season, 15 percent of guests (about one hundred thousand) activated their EpicMix accounts.[8] In the 2011–2012 season, more than two hundred thousand additional guests activated accounts and shared more than one million photos on their social networks.[9]

Besides adding value to the product offering, gamification can engage customers at different touch points. The Spanish bank BBVA created BBVA Game to encourage customers to use the bank's online services.[10] The game rewards players for completing challenges that are designed to educate them on using web banking, and encourages them to start using the service. Once players have accumulated points, they can exchange them for a variety of direct prizes or use the points to "purchase" tickets in lotteries for larger prizes. Customer benefits include the rewards offered for learning how to use web banking as well as the convenience of banking online. BBVA benefits from the cost reductions realized when customers choose to use online services rather than teller services. BBVA Game has eighty thousand users, of which 15 percent are referrals. The business results include a 5 percent increase in web-banking users and those users are spending 60 percent more time on the site.

One of the most common implementations of gamification in customer-focused applications provides opportunities for customers who act as brand advocates to more deeply engage and promote their favorite brands. Samsung Nation, a social loyalty program, rewards customers with points, levels, and badges for answering questions from other community members, watching product videos, or commenting on Samsung products. Samsung has seen a 66 percent increase in users and has more than quadrupled the number of answers to questions on the site. In addition, 34 percent of Samsung Nation users make purchases on the site, more than doubling the number of items placed in shopping carts.[11]

Building motivation into the product offering, changing customer interaction models, and driving deeper customer relationships are just a few of the ways that companies can leverage gamification in customer-focused solutions. Gamification is also being used to increase participation in market surveys, enhance conference experiences, and improve credit scores—and the list continues to grow.

To uncover opportunities to influence customer behaviors, organizations must evaluate prospects for incorporating gamification into the core products, leverage it in customer touch points, or create entirely new customer interaction models. It all starts with the simple question, "How can our customers be engaged and motivated to achieve their goals?"

GUIDING EMPLOYEES TO SUCCESS

Employee-focused applications are the fastest-growing area for gamification solutions, and the reason is not surprising. As I have already discussed, employee engagement is dismal in many organizations, which makes for a target-rich environment. There are countless opportunities to influence employees to change behaviors and improve results—both for the employee and the organization.

Like the employees of many IT organizations, the eight hundred IT staffers at DIRECTV had become risk averse and did not dare start innovative projects, nor did they share their failures so that others could learn from those mistakes. At the same time, employees were being asked to do more, and the end users' expectations were that technology should be fast, cheap, and frictionless. Something needed to be done to break down the fear barrier among IT staff and encourage risk taking, fast failures, and organizational learning. In order to take the DIRECTV IT group to the next level and gain strategic advantage, the company needed to encourage risk taking and sharing mistakes. According to Sven Gerjets, SVP of IT solutions delivery, "We needed to change the culture to de-demonize failure within the IT organization."[12]

To start this shift, DIRECTV launched a series of videos that encouraged employees to share project pitfalls and to help colleagues avoid making the same mistakes. But how could they get busy people to take time out of their days to watch videos? They had stumbled upon the idea of gamification, and seeing the success in other organizations, they decided to incorporate it into their solution. They created a gamified solution to motivate employees to watch the videos, share lessons learned, and drive a more risk-tolerant culture.

The solution is called F12: the "F" means "Fearless, Focused, Failure" and "12" represents the twelve commitments, including, "We admit fear of failure drives blame and erodes our performance" and "We can't succeed with fear in our hearts." These commitments were created to get IT staff to think differently and to promote a different language around failure. Using game mechanics and experience design, the solution encourages people to adopt new ways of working. Players are rewarded points for watching the videos, reading articles, and answering quiz questions. But, according to Sven Gerjets, "Those are the table stakes. We also have bonus point activities, because we wanted people to go from learning to acting differently." The solution also provides bonus points for activities like delivering a lunch-and-learn session or creating a video case study of lessons learned from a project that went awry.

As Russell Bacon, senior manager of IT metamorphosis at DIRECTV describes it, "We really wanted people to start teaching each other about their failures, making it safer to fail and creating an ecosystem of knowledge sharing." DIRECTV has created a "failure vault," in which 120 cases have been logged that the project management organization uses for "premortems" on projects. A premortem is a preventive approach designed to head off failure—at the outset of a project, the project teams review similar projects to understand the challenges they faced and avoid repeating any mistakes.

Players are guided from the basic level of passive learning through an active level of sharing lessons learned, to ultimately demonstrating the change. Staffers can nominate people who have really adopted the culture change for awards such as the "F12 Championship" and the "Collaboration Award."

One of the key aspects of the solution was to integrate internal social media platforms and sentiment analysis to understand how the solution was being perceived by the IT staffers. According to Bacon, "We've really used social to adjust our journey; we may do something different because of the feedback we get on social."

In fact, one of the early lessons the F12 team learned helped to guide the journey. In the first few weeks after the launch, about half the IT staff were active in F12, but the team wanted to drive higher participation, so they created the "Zero to Hero Award" for those players who had fewer than ten points in the game, to encourage more people to participate. The F12 team offered tickets to a hockey game to the top three new players who accumulated the most points over three days. On the surface, the incentive was a success, as participation ramped up to 75 percent. But analysis indicated sentiment around the F12 solution actually went down considerably. Digging deeper, they found that the people who were early adopters viewed this new award as a premium for nonparticipation. Clearly, this was not the message the team wanted to send, so they quickly introduced an "F12 Assistance" badge which was offered to people who helped other people get started in F12. Participation ramped up to almost 95 percent and the sentiment rose above previous levels. What they also found was that points and badges were actually more effective at driving behavior than the tangible reward of hockey tickets, proving the lesson learned from Dan Pink, that extrinsic rewards can actually have a negative effect.

Overall, the F12 solution has been a great success, not only in terms of adoption but, more importantly, in achieving the real goal. As Sven Gerjets related to me, "Ultimately, we're not measuring the success of the game; we're measuring the success of the culture shift." DIRECTV has seen an uptick in output and quality metrics. More qualitatively, the company is seeing risk taking depressurized and a shift in the language around failure. Gamification is a great approach for guiding people to change behaviors so they can become more effective, but it is not a great approach for getting people to make more widgets. If the problem is sheer production, then an incentive program with tangible rewards is probably the right answer. For example, sales organizations often use contests with prizes, like a trip to an exotic locale, for the top sales performers. This kind of incentive program can be effective in motivating the top performers to work a little harder. But gamification is not about motivating people to achieve the company's goals, it's about motivating people to achieve their own goals. Very few employees have a goal of working harder, but many employees are motivated to work better. And that's where gamification can be applied.

Often, getting people to work better is about getting them to adopt known success strategies. To achieve this behavior change, gamification can be integrated with processes to coach employees through the process execution, for example using gamification as a trigger to motivate salespeople to enter more detailed prospect information or to prompt them to call a client after a meeting. This approach provides more directed behavior change and can be useful in guiding employees in a more granular way through a process, helping to remedy issues in process execution.

Business travel offers an example of how gamification can improve a process. Many large organizations have implemented a managed travel program, with policies that attempt to balance the employee's travel preferences with the corporate objectives of reducing travel costs. But in some organizations, employees choose travel options that are not compliant with the corporate travel policies.

Now, some managed travel services leverage gamification to nudge business travelers into making better choices when they book their travel. As a business traveler reviews the travel options, he is rewarded with points and badges for selecting policy-compliant options. In some cases, those points can be accumulated and used to select noncompliant travel options when they are most meaningful to the traveler. In this way, both the organization's and the employee's goals are being met. Organizations can increase travel policy compliance while providing business travelers with the autonomy to select noncompliant options when they are most valuable to the traveler.

DRIVING SOCIAL COLLABORATION

Gamification and social media have a symbiotic relationship. As I mentioned earlier, gamified solutions are often linked to social media sites to amplify achievements, but the relationship also works the other way. Gamification can be used to drive social media adoption for collaboration both internally and externally.

Like many organizations, NTT Data struggled to drive adoption of its internal social collaboration platform. With sixty thousand professionals in thirty-six countries, it has tremendous opportunities to collaborate across the organization. To leverage these opportunities, NTT Data deployed a social network platform, called Socially, but the initial results were disappointing. After three months, only 250 employees were using the platform.

CTO Imran Sayeed decided to use gamification to drive adoption. Employees who participated in the site received "Karma Points," and could track their points on leaderboards. Adoption soared, with the user base exceeding forty-five hundred people within a few months and collaboration occurring across the United States, Canada, and India. Participants used the social media site to answer questions, share ideas, and locate experts in particular topic areas. Gamifying the solution was such a success that NTT Data created a gamification center of excellence, led by Naureen Meraj, whose background is in using games to encourage positive behavior modification.[13]

The NTT Data experience is not unique, and we are likely

just at the beginning of the fusion of gamification and social collaboration. Vendors are beginning to incorporate game mechanics into more popular platforms such as Microsoft SharePoint and IBM Connections, which will extend gamification to a large number of organizations.

Gartner believes the integration of gamification, social, and mobile increases the attractiveness, usability, and effectiveness of user-facing applications. In 2012, Gartner analyst Tom Austin predicted that, "In 2017, the majority of all new user-facing applications will exhibit gamified–social–mobile fusion."[14]

Gamification can play an important role in changing employee behaviors. As we have seen, organizations are already using gamification to change corporate culture, nudge people to comply with travel policy, and drive the adoption of social collaboration technologies. Other examples include driving sustainability, promoting safe working practices, and optimizing customer service and project performance. While this list keeps growing, Gartner also believes there is a huge opportunity to leverage gamification for change management.

My colleagues and I speak with organizations that use gamification as the primary method to transform business operations. However, successfully implementing change is hard. Dr. John Kotter, an expert on leading change, has "proven that 70 percent of all major change efforts in organizations fail. Why do they fail? Because organizations often do not take the holistic approach required to see the change through."[15]

Gamification can help implement change by defining a clear transformation path with simple steps and encouragement along the way. Change projects are anything but user-friendly. Commonly, change initiatives in organizations consist of overwhelming people with an intense training program in the new processes and applications, handing them a thick binder describing the new way of working, and sending them on their way with the promise of punishments for noncompliance. It's no surprise that success rates are dismal.

For change management, gamification takes a lesson from games. No one reads a manual to play Angry Birds. You simply start, and you develop skills as you progress. Gamifying change management is the same: this type of change effort recognizes that players must take small steps first and build their skills over time. The difficulty of the challenges increases as players develop skills, until they have fully implemented the change.

MOBILIZING COMMUNITIES FROM INTEREST TO ACTION

The American Heart Association (AHA) is a nonprofit organization dedicated to building healthier lives free of cardiovascular disease and stroke. The goal of the AHA is to improve the cardiovascular health of all Americans by 20 percent while reducing deaths from cardiovascular disease and stroke by 20 percent, by 2020. This will be achieved by funding research, providing public health education, supporting health-care professionals, and promoting healthy living. The AHA is funded primarily through contributions and fund-raising events.

In October 2010, the AHA began looking for innovative ways to engage communities with two objectives: to promote healthy living and to drive fund-raising. In February 2012, after reviewing a number of alternatives, the AHA decided to move forward with HeartChase, a set of gamified solutions to be used at special events organized by volunteers within the community and supported by the AHA.[16] The core HeartChase application is a mobile app that players use during the event. HeartChase is a fun way for players to engage in heart-healthy activities while raising funds to support the AHA.

HeartChase events turn the community into a playground, with teams of two to five players moving through ten checkpoints, all within a one-and-a-half- to two-mile radius of "game central." The event lasts for two hours, and during that time, all the teams compete to collect as many points as possible. A dynamically updated leaderboard displays each team's progress, which adds a level of competition to the game. According to Cami Thompson, national director of development and strategic planning at the AHA, "The leaderboard is constantly changing, and that boosts the competitive spirit and really motivates the players."

At each of the checkpoints, players must complete a heart-healthy activity to receive points. These activities are designed to be simple and fun, to help players take that first step toward making healthier choices. For example, a typical challenge might be for players to complete a Zumba dance routine. Once they have performed the activity, they scan a Quick Response (QR) Code to receive their points. Each event has checkpoints that, for example, may ask teams to answer questions, such as correctly guessing the sodium content of four foods on display. The numeric difference between the team's guess and the correct answer must be walked off by the team while wearing a pedometer.

In addition to the checkpoint challenges, there are one hundred hidden donation cards that teams must find and scan to win additional points. Typically, about one third of the donation cards are easily found, one third are more difficult, and one third are very difficult to find. These donation cards also appear on the map in the HeartChase app once they have been found.

Driven by volunteers, funds are raised from both players and community sponsors. Each team member is asked to raise at least $50 in donations in order to participate, but many players raise more, and teams raise additional funds to support the life-saving work of the AHA and to earn Game Advantages. Game Advantages give teams specific benefits during HeartChase game play, such as the ability to jump to the front of the line at a checkpoint or to make another team stop game play for five minutes and not earn points during that time. There are also many sponsorship opportunities for companies; the most common is to sponsor a checkpoint challenge. Checkpoint sponsorship allows a company to be involved in a unique way and gives it recognition through the HeartChase app when players complete the checkpoint.

HeartChase events are highly social activities. Not only the event but all the activities leading up to the event leverage social networks. Volunteers drive participation at the local level through word of mouth and social network feeds, such as Facebook, Twitter, and LinkedIn. A recruitment game board tracks progress against player/recruitment goals using progress bars and includes a countdown to the event.

Forty communities piloted HeartChase through June 2012 with great success. The gamified solution introduced players to easy and fun ways to improve their heart health, starting them on the journey to changing habits that have lasting effects. In a follow-up survey, players reported that they found new ways of maintaining healthy habits and, in some cases, achieved significant weight loss.

HeartChase is just one example of how gamification can be used to help motivate a community of interest to change behaviors and become a community of action. We have already seen one example from SickKids hospital, which engages patients to complete their pain reports, and yet another example from Free the Children, which uses We365 to engage youth in activities that have a positive social impact. The variety of applications is boundless.

Gamification can be used to motivate people to lose weight, stop smoking, or improve their fitness. And these are just a few examples that leverage gamification to help motivate people to change for the better. For example, MeYou Health has a number of gamified solutions that encourage people to make healthier choices and take concrete steps to improve their health. One of the solutions is a Daily Challenge, where participants receive an e-mail every day directing them to take one small step to improve their health, like taking the stairs or eating a healthy snack. Daily Challenge is just one of myriad of solutions that motivate people to adopt healthier habits.[17]

GAMIFIED STEPS TO CHANGE BEHAVIOR

Whether the target audience is customers, employees, or a community of interest, they are all people and they respond to similar stimuli for changing behaviors. These are common steps that can be applied to many different applications. Habits form over time and, once established, they can be difficult to change. The real issue is how to rewire our brains and replace old habits with new ones. At a detailed level, there are many different approaches to making new habits, but at a high level there are some common characteristics:

- Set goals
- Use triggers
- Take baby steps
- Find kindred spirits
- Enlist support from friends
- Build complexity over time
- Repeat until new habits are formed
- Keep it fresh

Let's examine each of these steps to understand how organizations have designed experiences that leverage game mechanics to lead people through the transformation journey.

Set goals. The first step in changing behaviors is to set a goal, one that meaningfully engages the players. For example, if the objective is to lose weight, then the goal may be to lose twenty pounds. Keeping an eye on the longer-term goal can help people take all of the small steps along the way. Try to imagine yourself in the skinny jeans that you haven't been able to wear in the last three years, and you will have a vision of what success looks like. Nike+ users can set up goals for NikeFuel, calories burned, running frequency, and/or distance. These goals can be shared to Facebook and Twitter, and the goals and progress appear every time a user logs onto the Nike+ website. HeartChase encourages participants and groups to set fund-raising goals. A gamified solution can provide the signposts on the road to success, marking your progress toward achieving the goal.

Use triggers. Until an action becomes part of a routine, people need to be reminded to make a change in their behavior. A gamified solution can provide those triggers by reminding players of the specific actions they need to take and when. For example, a gamified app running on your smartphone can remind you that it is time to take your medication or fill out your pain report, as we saw in the Pain Squad example. Gamified solutions set up triggers to start to change behaviors. The Nike+ SportWatch asks you if you are "ready for another run" if you haven't logged a run in five days. Opower sends e-mails or text messages to customers during peak-demand periods to encourage them to take measures to save energy.

Take baby steps. Often, when we think about making a change in our lives, we think in terms of big goals such as getting in shape or reducing energy consumption. And sometimes the enormity of the long-term goal is overwhelming, preventing us from even taking the first step. As the Chinese philosopher Laozi remarked, "A journey of a thousand miles begins with a single step."

The key to achieving larger goals is to break down the change into small, manageable steps. Opower suggests small changes with statements like, "Compact florescent lamps (CFLs) use 75 percent less energy and last six times longer than incandescent bulbs. Halogen lightbulbs and LEDs also provide high-quality illumination while cutting waste, so you can choose the efficient light that's best for your home."

Getting into shape is hard, but a simple concrete step, like taking the stairs instead of the escalator, is something we can manage. The Nike+ FuelBand users will collect more points for taking the stairs than the escalator. Once players have taken those first steps, moving toward the goal becomes easier. As Geoffrey, the veteran who wanted to lose weight, told me, his first run was less than a mile, but he continued and every run got easier and longer.

Find kindred spirits. Implementing change is hard work, but it is easier if you are part of a larger group of people who are also making the change. This works on a number of different levels. Changing the environment is critical to implementing change. When the people around you are doing something different, it is easier to make the same change in your own habits. It is part of human nature to want to be aligned with the people around you. Opower lets their users know they are in good company with messages like, "Saving energy is easy. We asked your neighbors. Seventy-seven percent of Palo Alto residents set their thermostats efficiently to save energy."

Surround yourself with people who are implementing the same change. You can also gain inspiration from those people who are ahead of you on the journey. Gamified solutions can be a tremendous help because they are not limited by the physical environment. You don't need to literally surround yourself with people going through the same change; you can do it virtually with a group of people using the same gamified solution. Nike+ lets you connect to friends on the Nike+ platform, ranks your position against your friends on a leaderboard, and allows you to challenge friends to achieve a goal or to work together to achieve group goals.

Enlist support from friends. Gamified solutions are often integrated with social media, which extends the reach of your support group to your friends on social media. Opower enables players to connect with their Facebook friends to compare energy usage, enter energy reduction competitions, and share energy-saving tips. Gamified solutions often post progress updates (with your permission) to your social circles. Nike+ can also connect to Facebook so your friends can cheer you on in real time.[18]

Build complexity over time. Most experts agree that change needs to start with simple steps, but more complex behaviors can be developed over time. BBVA Game, the Spanish bank's web banking learning solution, encourages players to start by watching instructional videos; they start out by trying some simple operations like checking account balances and doing basic transactions. As players develop skills and confidence, they move on to more complex operations like making transfers or paying bills. The gamified solution provides the coaching and guidance to lead people through processes gradually and put them on a path to more complex behavior change.

Repeat until new habits are formed. Once the new behavior is learned, it needs to be repeated over a period of time until a new habit is formed. When trying to reduce energy use, unplugging unused appliances or turning down your air conditioner requires some effort at first. But over time, thinking about energy conservation becomes a habit and people unconsciously turn off the lights when they leave a room and run the dishwasher during off-peak periods. Behavioral scientists may disagree about the number of repetitions or the time period that is required to form a new habit, but they agree on the need to repeat the new behavior until the habit is formed. As Geoffrey said, after he got started running with the Nike+ iPod sensor he couldn't stop, and he's still going strong after four years.

Keep it fresh. In some cases, the behavior change is a one-time event (e.g., quitting smoking) and once the new habit is formed, the goal is achieved and the player can stop using the gamified solution. In other cases, there are ongoing behavior changes that need to be made. To keep their solutions fresh, EpicMix continues to add new features every season, and Nike+ is constantly innovating and challenging players. In these cases of longer-term uses of a gamified solution, it is important to modify the solution to maintain interest—keeping it fresh.

Some solutions require a change in focus to respond to changing business needs, or, as is often the case in employee performance solutions, changes are required to focus on different aspects of the job over time. Sven Gerjets of DIRECTV recognizes the need for keeping the solution fresh: "You have to evolve the game or else it gets stale." Once employees have adopted a new set of habits, other areas may require attention, so the solution will evolve over time.

Change is hard, and gamification can be used to engage and motivate people to make behavioral changes in their lives. The examples illustrated in this chapter are just some of the most common applications. Almost daily, I have conversations with clients who are using gamification to change behaviors in new and different ways. We are just beginning to explore how gamification can be used to help people make positive changes in their lives. When you consider the possibilities, the opportunity is huge.

WRAP UP

✓ Customer-focused gamification solutions are far more than loyalty programs on steroids. Gamification can be used to add value to the product offering, change customer interaction models, and enable customer-support networks. Building gamification into customer touch points requires different thinking about what the customer values.

✓ Employee-focused applications are the fastest-growing area for gamification solutions and the opportunity is vast, from changing corporate culture, to directing employees to successful process execution, to implementing transformation programs. Employee-focused gamified solutions are changing the engagement model and value exchange between employer and employee.

✓ Gamification is particularly well suited to engaging communities of interest in changing behaviors. As we already know, the sweet spot for gamification is where there is overlap between player and organizational goals, and communities of interest exist because of shared goals.

✓ Gamification can play an important role in implementing change by defining a clear transformation path with simple steps and encouragement along the way. Gamification uses goal setting, triggers, and baby steps to help people change behaviors. Players can find kindred spirits and enlist the support of friends with social sharing. Gamification helps people repeat behaviors until they become habits, keep the process fresh, and develop change over time.

4
Using Gamification to Develop Skills

Learning happens every day and everywhere. Humans are hardwired to classify experiences and assimilate knowledge. We can almost effortlessly learn a new recipe or memorize a bus schedule. That's because the motivation is closely tied to the acquired skill or knowledge. The act of learning the recipe results in the satisfaction of a great meal, and learning a new bus schedule can reduce your wait times, so there is a clear line of sight between motivation and learning.

But sometimes learning is harder, particularly when the gratification of accomplishment is delayed. Spending years in school to prepare for a career is a long, hard slog. Corporate training is often dry, boring, and not easily connected to employees' goals. Whether it is formal education, corporate training, or informal learning, gamification can provide the path and add motivation to learning activities.

INSPIRING LEARNING AT KHAN ACADEMY

Tanis, a bright twenty-five-year-old woman, always struggled in school, and her teachers did little to build her self-esteem. In fact, Tanis was very intelligent and excelled in some areas, such as writing computer programs. But in her teens she was diagnosed with acute depression. As a result of her disease, she was scared of kids her own age and terrified of her teachers. Over time, she became disinterested in school, though she kept at it until she finished high school.

Initially, Tanis wanted to go to college. But since the students and teachers still terrified her, she lost interest in higher education as well. While her husband of eight years has always been very supportive of her and does whatever he can to make her feel safe, her disease has worsened over time. Eventually, she found it difficult to go out and stayed home most of the time.

In June 2012, Tanis discovered Khan Academy. The mission of Khan Academy is "to provide a free world-class education for anyone anywhere." It has a vast resource of educational materials and tools, with lessons delivered via YouTube videos and automated exercises that help students practice their newly learned skills until they achieve mastery.

At Khan Academy, Tanis received positive feedback that encouraged her continued learning. Nobody told her she was stupid. The software tapped into her computer skills, helping her become interested in physics and calculus. Once she mastered those, she moved on to learn mathematical probabilities. She found new meaning in her life and hope for the future.

At Khan Academy, each right answer wins some "energy points." When a student solves a series of problems quickly, she is rewarded with achievement badges. When she solves a string of ten problems in a row, she masters that lesson and can move on to the next. Students can see their progress as they master lessons on the knowledge map. The rewards, such as points and badges, are the hallmarks of gamification. But how can badges and points motivate people? The simple answer is that they don't. *It's what they mean* that motivates people. In Tanis's case, they meant progress toward reaching a seemingly impossible goal and, ultimately, the triumph of succeeding.

Tanis is hooked on learning and it's given her a purpose in life far beyond Khan Academy. She has spent time looking for a career where she can work in a quiet environment without the stress of dealing with a lot of other colleagues or the public. She has set a goal of becoming a data analyst. Khan Academy has given Tanis much more than math skills. It has boosted her self-esteem and has given her the confidence to escape the prison of her depression. In a letter to Salman Khan, the founder of Khan Academy, she writes:

> Thank you Sal. You've given me hope that I can actually follow my heart, and you've given me a way to no longer feel like a burden on my husband. You have helped me learn to smile, and be proud of myself when I "get" something. Words can't express how desperately thankful I am. Just, thank you Sal, thank you. I feel whole. I feel that I have self-worth. I've NEVER had that before. This is how you're saving my life.[1]

Tanis is a true demon slayer. While Tanis's challenges may be different from yours or mine, deep down, each and every one of us dreams about becoming better, overcoming challenges, and achieving our goals. Gamification can provide the push to take that first step, as well as the motivation and guidance to achieve your goals.

MASTERY FOR THE MASSES

Salman Khan is not a teacher, nor has he been trained in teaching. His interest in tutoring students started as an undergrad at MIT where he tutored students at a nearby school. A few years later he began tutoring again with his cousin Nadia, a sixth-grade student at the time. Nadia was doing very well in school, but she began to struggle with math. Sal was working as a hedge fund analyst at the time, and he offered to tutor his cousin remotely. Starting by tutoring a single student and then moving on to other family and friends, Salman Khan eventually founded Khan Academy in 2008, advancing the work he had been doing over the previous four years. In 2010, Khan Academy received large grants from Google and the Bill and Melinda Gates Foundation, and the organization began to grow. Khan Academy is focused primarily on helping K–12 students by providing short educational videos and exercises that enable learners to practice newly acquired skills until they have mastered them.

According to Sal Khan, gamification is an important part of the approach to engaging students in learning at Khan Academy. In fact, Sal told me the game mechanics actually predate the video tutorials. Energy points are collected for the successful completion of various activities on the website. Badges are awarded for completing lessons and viewing videos and other activities. Detailed statistics on activities and skills progress over time are provided to Khan Academy users. The staff at Khan Academy analyzes the interaction cycles to ensure that game mechanics provide continuing motivation to students.

Currently Khan Academy has about fifty-one staff members and continues to build its video library of tutorials (more than five thousand) and practice problems (more than one hundred thousand). The Khan Academy website is visited by about ten million unique viewers every month, who collectively have watched more than three hundred million videos. Over 1.6 billion exercises have been completed, and that number continues to grow at a rate of about four million per day.[2]

In an early pilot, Khan Academy worked with seventh-grade students who struggled with math. When students used the Khan Academy tutorials, there was a shift in performance across the entire spectrum of student skill levels. The study found a significant reduction in the number of students with below basic skills and a significant increase in students with skills at a proficient or advanced level.

But Khan Academy is just one example of an organization that is mobilizing to develop skills in a broad community of interest. NASA has partnered with the Center for Educational Technologies (CET) to motivate students to learn STEM areas (science, technology, engineering, and mathematics) and recognize achievements with badges.[3] For example, learners at the CET site can earn a "NASA Lunar Rover Geometry Badge" for using geometry to calculate the shortest distance for the Lunar Rover Vehicle to complete three tasks.[4] Increasingly organizations such as P2P University and Coursera are awarding certified badges to learners to demonstrate achievements. Badges are microcredentials that let employers understand the skills and knowledge that a prospective employee has acquired in both formal and informal training activities.

Gamification helps drive engagement and motivate people in many different learning situations. There are as many gamified training opportunities as there are communities of interest. Some examples are:

- **U.S. government.** The Department of Health and Human Services has deployed a gamified solution to educate healthcare practitioners on best practices surrounding privacy and security.[5]
- **Duolingo.** A free language-learning website, Duolingo uses gamification to engage users in learning a second language while at the same time translating the web.[6]
- **Wall Street Survivor.** This gamified solution teaches potential investors how to invest in the stock market without risking real money.[7]

ENERGIZING EMPLOYEE TRAINING

Gamification in learning is moving beyond formal education and expanding rapidly into the corporate training environment. Imran Sayeed, CTO at NTT Data, told me that "corporate training is one of the areas where gamification is getting the most traction with the client base."[8] But NTT Data is also leveraging gamification internally.

With more than sixty-thousand employees, many of them located at customer sites, NTT Data faces a challenge in identifying and training leaders. Consultants may be working at customer sites for years or even decades, and over time they can begin to feel disconnected from the organization. NTT Data wanted to recognize employees for their skills, learning, and achievement and ensure they maintained a solid connection to the company.

In 2012, NTT Data launched the Ignite Leadership game specifically to identify leaders and develop their skills. The solution leverages game mechanics and design to engage employees in the learning process. In the first year that the program was in place, seven hundred employees participated. The solution starts with an assessment of the employee's knowledge in five critical management areas: negotiation, communication, time management, change management, and problem solving. The intent is to determine people's strengths and weaknesses and to tailor the learning to focus on building weak areas and develop well-rounded leaders.

Training is based on an experiential learning process in which learners are given real-world-scenario-based questions and some choices for actions to take in the given scenario. There is no one right answer; rather, there are multiple options, though one selection might be better than the others. The design team felt that knowledge retention would be better if the employee experienced the scenario rather than simply asking questions and getting answers. Analytics of the employee's progress are shared with her manager, and in this way, the managers can identify when employees are struggling with a particular topic and provide additional support.

Training is structured as a journey, and players receive points and badges, progressing through levels. A leaderboard shows players how they stack up against their team members and in the overall ranking. The solution also connects to Socially, the corporate collaboration platform described earlier in this book, which allows people to collaborate on different leadership topics.

One innovative collaboration approach NTT Data has built into the solution is called "sharepoints," which players can award to others in the game to recognize their effort and achievements in leadership development.

Surprise trivia questions, another unique feature, pop up at random in the game. Questions may be about a global strategy, a new acquisition, or anything that pertains to the company as a whole. Senior managers provide the questions, which gives players a connection to people they may not otherwise interact with—and adds an element of serendipity to the solution. According to Naureen Meraj, NTT's senior global director of gamification and strategic engagement, "This is a way for senior leaders to participate in the game and have an investment in potential future leaders." Because players never know when a senior manager may ask a question, they are motivated to check in to the system regularly.

The program is still in the pilot stage but the results are positive. So far, fifty people in the program have taken on leadership roles, which is an increase of 50 percent over the standard path. Players have contributed 220 ideas for improvements in customer accounts and thirty ideas for existing projects through the "Smart Idea Challenge." People in the program are also recommending NTT Data to their peer networks, resulting in a 30 percent increase in referrals. Leadership program participants demonstrate an increase in employee satisfaction and a decrease in attrition rates.

CAPTIVATING THE CUSTOMER

Expanding customer skills using gamification is an area just starting to be explored. In the cases where gamification has been used to increase customer knowledge, the projects have focused on situations where customers need to overcome a steep learning curve in order to use a product or service effectively. Health care in the United States provides an example.

Research by Carnegie Mellon University reveals that only 14 percent of Americans understand basic insurance concepts such as deductible, co-pay, coinsurance, and out-of-pocket maximum. The research draws on two surveys of Americans between the ages of twenty-five and sixty-four who have private health insurance.[9] And the problem will only get worse. As the Affordable Care Act compels more American individuals and families to purchase health care through the exchanges, millions of people who may have never had health insurance will scramble to understand the exchanges, learn how to select health insurance, and figure out how to use their plans more effectively.

Health-care plan members are being asked to make complex decisions on health care, and currently most of the material used to educate them is delivered as text-based booklets or web pages. These materials get used in the open-enrollment period over a couple of weeks each year. Often, there is no ongoing educational material to help members understand how to use their benefits more effectively. A lot of new benefits types are being introduced, and members are being asked to pay more out of their pockets. A better approach to health plan education was needed.

Organizations like Capital BlueCross, partnering with Change Healthcare Corporation, are providing help to educate members on the complexities of health insurance. Healthcare University is a gamified solution that provides a series of courses designed to help members gain a better understanding of health insurance and benefits, and to become smarter health-care consumers.[10]

Change Healthcare launched Healthcare University in April 2013 with five subject areas and four or five short courses per area. The five subject areas include:

1. Health Insurance 101—a course on health insurance basics that teaches members about basic terminology.
2. Benefits Selection—this covers topics such as understanding the difference between HMOs and PPOs.
3. Ways to Save—this course addresses topics such as switching from a branded drug to a generic drug, going from a thirty-day to a ninety-day prescription, or selecting an outpatient imaging center for an MRI.
4. Billing—a module that provides education on how to become your own health-care advocate.
5. Health Insurance Marketplaces—an introduction to the exchanges that launched as part of the Affordable Care Act.

The courses are built around short (two- or three-minute) animated videos that explain the concepts, followed by a five-question quiz that unlocks a game. Players earn points for registering and for each of the activities in the course (watching the video, taking the quiz, or playing the game). There is also a leaderboard, where players can see how they compare with other members. When the player completes all the courses within the subject area, he earns a badge. The badges give players a sense of reward and progress through the product, and encourage the players to continue on the journey to become educated health-care consumers.

Blue Cross and Blue Shield of Minnesota launched a pilot focused on its internal workforce of about thirty-five hundred employees. Over the six-week pilot period, progress was closely tracked to understand whether the gamified solution engaged the employees in the topics. The result was that nearly 40 percent of employees registered for the training. In the initial launch, players had access to only two of the subjects, or ten courses. Over the six-week period, players, on average, completed eight of the ten courses. Looking at the activity, there was a high level of engagement. On average, each user completed twenty-seven actions in the product during the pilot period. Employees watched more than nine thousand videos, took about seventy-five hundred quizzes, and played almost twenty thousand games.

A user satisfaction study was done at the end of the pilot period, and of the fourteen hundred employees who registered, four hundred gave feedback and scored the gamified solution A- overall. One unexpected result was the really high quiz scores, about 98 percent average. As Clayton Nicholas, Change Healthcare's VP of strategy and marketing explained to me, "Once the players saw their names on the leaderboard and understood that they were being ranked against their peers, they actually watched the educational videos two or three times so that when they took the quiz they could get higher scores and earn more points."[11] That reinforces the value of the education.

Gamification is also being used in training materials for products that require customers to gain basic skills before being able to use the products effectively. One example is Autodesk, which provides complex software for use in 3D design, engineering, and entertainment. One of the challenges the company faces is the knowledge gap that trial users must overcome to really begin to use the software. Autodesk developed a gamified solution to get trial users of its 3ds Max product up to speed quickly. By leading people through a series of tutorials, trial users could quickly on-board and gain an understanding of the power of the tool. Autodesk was able to achieve a 10 percent increase in downloads and a 40 percent increase in trial use.[12]

GAMIFYING SKILLS DEVELOPMENT

Gamification and learning are a natural fit. As we learned from Dan Pink's book *Drive*, mastery is a strong motivator. We all have an innate desire to improve. People are often inspired to work toward mastering a particular skill or building their knowledge. The challenge is not getting people to want to learn and grow—they already do—it is helping them find the path to success. The solution is to break the learning process into small steps, so that every step stretches the player's abilities but is still within her reach. Only then can she complete the journey and achieve her goal. While there is a lot of variation in how gamification is applied to learning, the common steps typically applied include:

- Define the goal
- Break down the steps
- Check for dependencies
- Create theory/practice engagement loops
- Recruit mentors and collaborators
- Celebrate success

Define the goal. Ralph Waldo Emerson famously said, "Life is a journey, not a destination." But the journey is filled with waypoints. We may not know what the destination is, but we need to know the next waypoint. Setting your goal to the next waypoint provides clarity and purpose to your journey. As we saw in the NASA example, players are offered a goal to achieve a "NASA Lunar Rover Geometry Badge" for using geometry to calculate the shortest distance for the Lunar Rover Vehicle to complete three tasks. When learning a new skill or acquiring knowledge, having a clearly defined goal is crucial to success.

Break down the steps. Gamification takes players on a journey, balancing skills they are developing with the level of challenge that the game presents. You can think of this as a script, with the relevant parts of the story being added over time; as the complexity of the material progresses, the player is building upon material learned previously. The learners in NTT Data's Ignite Leadership game go on a journey to develop their leadership skills, particularly in areas where they are weak. Progress is marked with points and punctuated with levels and badges.

Check for dependencies. Learning is a progressive activity, with skills and knowledge building upon previously learned material. We must be sure there are no gaps in learning that will hinder students in subsequent material. In his book, *The One World Schoolhouse*, Salman Khan refers to these gaps as "Swiss cheese learning." He uses calculus as an example of "the most common subject on which students meet their Waterloo. This is not because calculus is fundamentally difficult. It is because calculus is a synthesis of much that has gone before." Understanding those fundamental concepts builds a strong foundation for learning more advanced topics. Khan Academy uses a knowledge map to identify topics and their dependencies.

Create theory/practice engagement loops. Gamification uses engagement cycles, which provide players with instruction, a challenge, and feedback on their attempts to complete the challenge. For example, Khan Academy students are first presented with a short video that explains the topic, such as a mini-lecture on basic division. Then learners are presented with a division problem to solve. The player attempts to solve the problem and is provided with immediate feedback—if the answer is incorrect, the button shakes "No," but if the answer is correct, a smiley face appears and some "leaves" are earned. Gamification breaks the learning process into small, achievable steps and provides constant feedback and encouragement throughout the process.

NTT Data takes a different approach, in that it asks learners a question and provides them with multiple-choice answers. There is no one right answer, but some are better than others. Rather than gaining knowledge through theoretical lectures, learners acquire knowledge through experience and discussion with peers and mentors. The approach is to engage learners through doing—experiential learning.

Experiential learning is contrasted with other forms of conceptual learning. There is considerable debate on which approach is best for which types of learner and for the subject area being addressed. It is clearly beyond the scope of this book to engage in that debate. I will simply say that there are many different learning theories that can be implemented in a gamified solution, but the most commonly applied method is the conceptual learning approach described in the Khan Academy, BBVA Game, and Healthcare University examples. The NTT Data and Duolingo examples, however, successfully employ an experiential learning approach. Wall Street Survivor combines the experiential and conceptual learning approaches.

Recruit mentors and collaborators. Learning is best done in a collaborative environment, and most gamified learning solutions encourage learners to develop a network of peers or enlist a tutor to engage and enhance the learning process. NTT Data's solution encourages peer collaboration by connecting to the corporate social collaboration platform and uses "sharepoints" to build bonds between learners.

In traditional educational models, the teacher lectures in the classroom and assigns homework so that students can practice the lessons learned. The challenge with this model is that there is little time for teachers to provide one-on-one help for students who are struggling with a particular topic. Khan Academy uses a model of "flipping the classroom," where the lectures and practice time can be assigned as homework and the classroom time is devoted to teachers helping students work through challenges.

Khan Academy also enables teachers, parents, tutors, or peers to become "coaches," who can monitor a student's progress, see what badges they have been awarded, and to encourage them to continue learning.

Celebrate success. Learning is a lifelong process, but milestones come regularly. Recognizing achievements is important for maintaining engagement. In gamification, achievements are recognized in a number of ways, with one of the more common ways being badges. Badges are used in all types of gamification solutions (including behavior change and driving innovation) but they have a special meaning in developing skills because these badges represent microcredentials that can be used to certify skills attainment.

One of the challenges of badges in learning is that they are most often only recognized by the issuing organization, and they are difficult for others to verify. But that is starting to change. Mozilla and the MacArthur Foundation have launched the Open Badges project, which provides the technical infrastructure to support issuing, earning, and displaying badges. Learners can earn badges that recognize achievements both inside and outside the classroom. Badges are collected in a "backpack" that allows learners to display their achievements on digital platforms such as social networks. The badge infrastructure offers interested viewers such as employers or educators the opportunity to click on the badge to verify the issuer and the criteria for achievement.

Gamification has proven to be an effective method to engage people in learning activities. This will become even more important as more learning activities move to digital delivery. Gamification is just one of a number of forces that are reshaping the way we learn. Training and education are primed for a transformational change.

WRAP UP

✓ Gamification motivates people during the long process of learning and extends the classroom to provide learning opportunities to geographically dispersed students of varying abilities.

✓ Gamified solutions break the learning process into small steps, so that every step stretches the player's abilities, but it is still within his reach.

✓ Learning is best done in a collaborative environment, and most gamified learning solutions encourage learners to develop a network of peers or enlist a tutor to engage and enhance the learning process.

✓ Learning is a progressive activity, with skills and knowledge built upon previously learned material. Gamified solutions must leave no gaps in learning that will hinder students in approaching subsequent material.

✓ Gamified solutions can implement either conceptual or experiential learning approaches, or a combination of both.

✓ Badges and other rewards have a special meaning in developing skills because they represent microcredentials that can be used to certify skills attainment.

5

Using Gamification to Drive Innovation

The days when innovation was assigned to a small group of big brains are over. Organizations have moved to a crowd-sourced model for innovation. Leveraging the wisdom of the crowd brings many perspectives to the innovation challenge, and each represents a unique point of view that sees the problem differently. But how does a crowd innovate?

Left to their own devices, people will optimize their condition within the constraints of the environment. This optimization is constant and can be seen in the way people perform tasks at work, select investments in the stock market, or make their daily commute to the workplace, to name just a few examples. Scientists call this phenomenon "emergence," and it is quite the opposite of the central planning of big brains. It is the collective actions of many individuals, constrained by rules, who self-organize into complex, adaptive systems, often with radically novel results. Take the stock market as an example of an emergent system. The market goes up or down because of the collective action of many individual investors operating within the rules. The invisible hand described by Adam Smith is actually the collective actions of many people, and it is an emergent system. Stock markets leverage the wisdom of the crowd for the efficient allocation of capital.

Gamification can provide the structure to engage, motivate, and focus the innovation activities of the crowd, whether they are employees, customers, or communities of interest. Gamified innovation solutions provide players with the play space and create the objectives, rules, rewards, and other aspects of the player engagement model, but they don't define the outcome—players are free to innovate within that space.

IDEA GENERATION AT THE DWP

The United Kingdom's Department for Work and Pensions (DWP) is responsible for welfare and pension policy, and is a key player in tackling child poverty. It is the biggest public-service delivery department in the UK, and with more than 100,000 people on staff, the DWP has a tremendous human resource to draw on for innovation. The challenge has been to harness all that creativity at the front line and develop ideas into a meaningful set of potential projects that can be implemented. According to David Cotterill, director of innovation, "People wanted to help make things better, and all we had to do was create a structured way for them to do that while providing them with an incentive to do so. The gaming aspect is that incentive."

DWP created a market for ideas called "Idea Street" that employees could contribute to and collaborate in, and where they could gain recognition for their participation in innovation.[1] Launched in 2008 and built on Spigit's enterprise innovation platform, DWP incorporated game mechanics into Idea Street with the intention of creating an environment employees would find engaging.

By applying game mechanics to the innovation problem, DWP developed an innovation market that enabled employees to participate in innovation, rewarding them using a point system. The points, called DWPeas, are awarded for idea generation and for contributions through all stages of development. Employees can contribute their ideas, develop the ideas of others, and even use their DWPeas to invest in the ideas they find most promising. When an idea is selected for implementation, the "shareholders" are rewarded with more DWPeas. Conversely, these same share-holders can lose DWPeas for ideas that are not selected for implementation. The result is an active market of ideas that employees are working on. The market even includes a "buzz index" that highlights the ideas that are most actively discussed. For example, if an idea submitted by an employee causes the buzz index to soar, other employees will be drawn into commenting or contributing to the development of the idea. Teams with promising ideas often recruit managers with budget authority who can be involved in idea development and, ultimately, help gain investment. In cases where no one on the team can take the idea to the next level, the innovation team shepherds the idea to the appropriate manager for review.

Employees are highly engaged in Idea Street. The initial implementation of Idea Street drew approximately forty-five hundred users and generated about fourteen hundred ideas, of which sixty-three have gone forward to implementation within the first eighteen months. Employees want to be on the inside of the most promising ideas, which drives ongoing participation. The idea market itself provides a scoring system to evaluate the most promising ideas, as players will invest only in the ideas they believe will be selected for implementation. Game mechanics have been effectively employed to turn Idea Street into an engaging player-centric experience.

Idea Street provides DWP's management with a ranked portfolio of well-developed ideas that they can select from for implementation. In the first eighteen months, DWP has invested in projects with returns totaling £21 million (34 million USD) in benefits. The motivation for employees is increased recognition and a feeling that their contributions are making a difference. In one project, a DWP call center employee submitted and developed an idea for creating internal marketing material using a network of talented employees already on board. The idea was adopted, and the employee who submitted and shepherded the idea through the process was invited to work on a temporary assignment in the office of the permanent secretary (head) of DWP, gaining insights into the inner workings at the top level of the organization.

In April 2012, DWP redeveloped the application and relaunched the innovation management platform. In the updated idea-generation process, employees' crowdsourced that are supported by the community move up a leaderboard; the top ideas are passed along to idea mentors who work with the teams to develop the ideas. The relaunch was supported by a large marketing effort and by senior management, and the results are impressive. In the eight months since the relaunch, fifty-seven thousand employees have signed up to the community and have submitted a total of fifty-seven hundred ideas, of which more than five hundred have been successful and seventeen hundred are under consideration.[2]

PRODUCT DEVELOPMENT AT QUIRKY

People are naturally creative and eager to express themselves. Innovation can go beyond employees to an entire community of interest. Quirky, a crowdsourcing product development company, engages a community of inventors and designers to submit, develop, and refine ideas for new consumer products. Leveraging the collective intelligence of more than six hundred thousand members, the community provides the ideas and Quirky provides the infrastructure and support to engineer, produce, and distribute the products. Since starting in 2009, Quirky has launched more than four hundred products.[3]

From the "broom groomer"—a dustpan that cleans the dust bunnies from the broom—to "props"—the headphone keepers—to "stem"—a citrus spray head that you stick right into the lemon—the products are *quirky*. Inventors come from all different backgrounds, and the only qualifications are having great ideas and collaborating to make a product real.

Quirky uses "influence" as a point system. Influence translates directly into a share of the royalties for products that are launched. Community members earn influence for their contribution to product development. The largest share of influence is awarded to the inventors who submit winning product ideas, but smaller shares can be earned by participants who vote up the best ideas, collaborate in the development of the product, suggest and vote on product names, or play the "pricing game." Once a product idea has been selected to launch, it's marked with a "We're making this" badge. Each idea has thousands of contributors who shape the product from idea to launch. Quirky is a great example of an emergent game that leverages the creative talents of a large community, using a market game construct where influence is the currency.

The process is sticky. In the course of writing this book, I joined the Quirky community and poked around to see how it worked (at Gartner, we call this "research"). While I didn't have any great consumer product ideas to submit off the top of my head, I did see some interesting ideas in development. One was an "anti-theft rucksack," and Quirky was evaluating names for the rucksack. So I went through a selection of names that had already been submitted and chose the names I preferred, building influence along the way. Going one step further, I submitted a name of my own—the "Saf-T-Sac"—to compete with the other fourteen hundred ideas that had already been submitted. Watching my submission bounce up and down in the ranking was captivating, and I was hooked.

BARCLAYCARD RING GAMIFIES CUSTOMER COCREATION

Gartner defines customer cocreation as a collaborative initiative between companies and their customers, enabling the joint design of products and services. These initiatives include the creation of goods, services, and experiences—companies amplify their results by drawing on clients' intellectual capital. On Gartner's 2013 Hype Cycle for Digital Banking, customer cocreation is in the "technology trigger" phase. In other words, it is on the bleeding edge.

In April 2012, Barclaycard combined customer cocreation with gamification and launched an entirely new kind of credit card called Barclaycard Ring. Barclaycard was responding to three disruptive forces: (1) trust in U.S. banks was very low, (2) banking regulators were pushing for simplicity, transparency, and fairness, and (3) the explosion of social media created an opportunity to engage customers. Responding to these factors, the bank decided to leverage the wisdom of the crowd in a new way. The result was a simple credit card, with no rewards and no teaser rates. Rather, it has a simple structure and a low rate of 8 percent. Compared to the average rate of 15 percent on U.S. credit cards, the idea was off to a good start.

One of the real differences was the transparency of the product. The Barclaycard Ring product operates as a separate profit center, and profits generated by the community are shared with the community. The community votes on what to do with the profit: to give it back to community members in the form of a statement credit, to aggregate it and put it toward a charitable contribution, or to combine these two options. Barclaycard shares monthly financials and provides a detailed annual report for the Ring card with the community, detailing the income, expenses, and profit. Members can see clearly where profits are allocated to marketing, shareholders, and taxes, as well as the portion of Giveback that goes to the card members and to the charities they have selected. As Paul Wilmore, managing director of consumer markets for Barclaycard U.S., told me, "It's a level of transparency that no other bank has either been willing or able to show to its cardholders."[4] Community members have a real stake in making the card product work better, and that changes the way they think about their credit card and their behavior.

For example, in October 2012, Barclaycard asked the Ring community if the company should change its late-fee policy. The existing policy allowed members a three-day grace period before charging a late-payment penalty. Barclaycard proposed eliminating the three-day grace period and allowing one late payment per year. From its analysis, Barclaycard estimated it would generate 15 percent more late-fee revenue, which would result in higher profits for the community. Members voted overwhelmingly to adopt the policy. They were willing to punish those members who were habitually late payers to generate more profit for the community. This behavior may seem counterintuitive, but because most members paid their bills on time, they wouldn't be adversely affected. And many wanted to generate more profit for the community. When customers were asked to share in both the decision making and benefits of those decisions, they behaved more like shareholders than customers.

Gamification is used by Barclaycard to motivate members to participate in the development of the community. Members gain status for participating in the community by suggesting and voting on ideas for how to improve the product. There are five status tiers: bronze, silver, gold, platinum, and palladium, and every member's status is visible to the community, adding weight to their contributions.

Members are also awarded badges for actions such as going paperless, contributing to the community, or recruiting new members. A multicolored ring acts as a progress bar to show a member's involvement in the community and product. Barclaycard has also created an invitation-only experts section, where expert members get sneak peeks at new product features and act as an advisory board, providing feedback on introducing new things to the community. Barclaycard Ring has about twenty thousand members: about half are "active voyeurs," while about 10 percent are active contributors to the community.

HOW GAMIFICATION SPURS INNOVATION

Gamified innovation solutions tend to be competition based. These solutions differ from those designed to motivate behavior change and skills development, which are more commonly collaborative. The reason is simple: when organizations are looking for innovative ideas, they often need to identify a small number of the best ideas, so a competitive structure works well.

Gamification can leverage the following set of approaches to innovation solutions:

- Enlist players
- Solicit ideas
- Select ideas
- Develop ideas
- Get to launch

Enlist players. To leverage the wisdom of the crowd in innovation, organizations first need to get the crowd engaged, motivated, and focused. A critical mass of players is required for crowdsourced innovation solutions to be successful, and building the player base will require some effort. For example, the DWP discovered they needed to attract about 5 percent of the employee base to Idea Street to reach critical mass. To do that, a marketing campaign was launched to encourage players to sign in to Idea Street. Once critical mass is achieved, the solution can take off as the players will attract new players and the solution can go viral. Encouraging players to join is particularly important in employee-facing solutions, as sometimes employees need to overcome the mind-set that participation in innovation is not part of their job. Management must provide strong support to encourage people to participate.

Once the players get onto the gamified innovation platform, we find that people's goals naturally align with participating in innovation in a couple of different ways. Making people part of the change gives them a sense of autonomy. Employees naturally want to have a say in how the organization will evolve.

The same is true for customer- and community-facing solutions. Barclaycard Ring members are motivated to collaborate in the community to drive changes to the card product. After all, they are stakeholders and are going to be directly affected by the result. As we saw in the Quirky example, the process of getting an invention to market is complex, and collaborating in projects gives members a sense that they are part of something larger than themselves.

Solicit ideas. Idea generation is a creative process, and the target audience must be encouraged to submit bold ideas. In most gamified innovation solutions, idea submission is rewarded with a large share of points, shares, influence, or whatever rewards element is in use. As we saw in the Quirky example, the largest share of influence is awarded to the inventor who submits a winning product idea. The same is true in DWP's Idea Street.

Players who submit ideas play a special role in innovation solutions. They are typically seen as the "owner" of the idea, and are the ones who drive support and development of the idea. When soliciting ideas, organizations need to think about putting boundaries around the ideas. It is generally a good plan to have a broad innovation space and audience, with some boundaries that focus the ideas. Quirky, for example, is looking for inventions in the consumer product area, while DWP is looking for ideas that apply to its process and service portfolio, and Barclaycard Ring is looking for ideas that apply to one specific credit card product.

Select ideas. The power of the crowd really starts to show in idea selection. In this phase, ideas are evaluated and voted on by community members to ensure that the best ideas bubble to the top. In the Quirky and Barclaycard Ring examples, members are asked to vote up new ideas. In the DWP approach, employees can invest in the ideas they think are most promising. This voting stage is usually time blocked, to make the submission and selection process dynamic. Regardless of the approach taken, the community needs to drive the idea-selection process. The advantage of this approach is that it leverages the wisdom of the crowd to evaluate and select the best ideas from a large number of submissions.

Develop ideas. One of the principal challenges that innovators or inventors face is that they lack many of the skills required to develop an idea to the point where it can be considered for launch. This is where members of the community can contribute their unique talents to develop the ideas. In the Quirky example, there is a structured process for developing an invention that can involve thousands of community members in decisions about design, product names, and pricing. In the DWP example, teams form around ideas and develop them to the point where they can be evaluated for launch. In all cases, community-driven development enables people to contribute to ideas that are not their own and build a better proposal.

Get to launch. At some point, the rubber meets the road and real money has to be invested in taking an idea to the next step. Different organizations use different approaches that are aligned with internal investment and governance processes, but all organizations need to ensure that an appropriate process is in place to take innovations from the idea stage to the project stage. In the DWP example, the manager of the business unit that will eventually "sponsor" the innovation must champion the idea.

In the Quirky example, the community discusses and votes on ideas to take to production. In the Barclaycard Ring example, Barclaycard reviews community-selected ideas and determines which should move forward, and sometimes the community is asked to vote on idea adoption.

One word of caution: community members must have confidence that their ideas are being seriously considered and at least some of the "winning" ideas need to move forward and ultimately be implemented. The organization risks losing community confidence if ideas are not taken forward or if they languish for too long before decisions are made. The decision-making process must be as transparent as possible to instill confidence in the community members that their ideas are being considered in a fair and open manner.

As you can see, the wisdom of the crowd is a potent force for innovation, but it needs to be engaged and focused. Gamification benefits innovation by engaging the crowd in idea-generation and development activities. It creates a play space where innovation can occur and offers guidance to focus idea generation. It orchestrates innovation to benefit the enterprise.

WRAP UP

- ✓ Gamified innovation solutions tend to be competition based. These differ from behavior change and skills development solutions, which lean to being more collaborative.
- ✓ Gamification can provide the structure to engage, motivate, and focus the innovation activities of the crowd and leaves players free to innovate within that space.
- ✓ Sometimes people need to overcome the mind-set that participation in innovation is not part of their job. Management must provide strong support to encourage people to participate.

- ✓ In most gamified innovation solutions, idea submission is rewarded with a large share of points, shares, influence, or whatever rewards element is in use.
- ✓ The power of the crowd really starts to show in idea selection. In this phase, ideas are evaluated and voted on by community members to ensure that the best ideas bubble to the top.
- ✓ The community is critical in developing ideas to the point where they can be launched as projects. Community members can help fill the skills gaps of the originator of the idea and collaboratively develop the most valuable ideas.
- ✓ Community members must have confidence that their ideas are seriously considered and that at least some of the "winning" ideas will more forward to become implemented projects.

PART II

DESIGNING A GAMIFIED PLAYER EXPERIENCE

6

Player-Centric Design

Experiences are personal encounters that occur over a period of time and can deeply impact our perceptions, build our knowledge, and direct our actions. In a gamified solution, the player experience is designed as a journey and takes place in a play space that may encompass both the physical and virtual worlds. When I say design, I am not referring to technical design; rather, I am referring to experience design. While technical design is important, the focus here is on the more challenging work of designing the player experience. Additionally, *experience* design is not the same as *user experience* design, which focuses on the human–computer interface, although those designers may form part of the team. In fact, experience design is entirely different from a typical software design approach and requires a different set of skills to be successful. It draws on the disciplines of design thinking, behavioral science, and emergent systems.

PLAYER EXPERIENCE DESIGN PROCESS

The player experience design process breaks down the steps to building a gamified application and structures the tasks in a logical order. It focuses the design on achieving player goals and reduces both the time and the risks of designing a gamified solution.

FIGURE 6–1: Player Experience Design Process

Over the next two chapters we will illustrate the steps of the design process by examining how YakTrade, a fictitious discount brokerage, develops a gamified solution to take social investing to the next level.

YakTrade a U.S.-based online brokerage, targets under-forty individual investors. Its clients are not older, high-net-worth individuals looking for staid financial institutions; rather, they are tech-savvy individuals growing their portfolios and looking for a brokerage that understands them. YakTrade's strategy is to focus on this next generation of wealth builders. YakTrade is a young company for a young market. Launched in 2009, when investors had lost all faith in financial markets, many people doubted Yak-Trade would survive, but CEO Melissa Green saw things differently.

First of all, in 2009, there was no place for markets to go but up, and while other discount brokerages were in cost-cutting mode, YakTrade was in growth mode. Its target client base was just getting started as investors and had not been badly burned in the crash of 2008.

Second, the lack of trust in traditional brokerages became an advantage for the company. YakTrade lacked the resources to provide research, but investors had become highly skeptical of professional advice, so it didn't matter much. Because the major discount brokerages had trained their clients to expect research, it was a cost they would continue to have to bear, giving YakTrade a cost advantage.

Third, YakTrade's younger investors have a different perspective on personal financial management. They don't think that discussions about investing should be hushed, private conversations with a personal financial advisor. Younger investors want to be part of a community of like-minded people, and that's what YakTrade provides.

Yakker is YakTrade's private social media platform. Similar to Facebook, Yakker lets YakTrade clients share ideas, investment strategies, and advice within the community. It is what CEO Melissa Green calls "social investing"—a virtual version of the community spirit that flourishes in traditional face-to-face investment club meetings.

Finally, the younger generation that YakTrade targets is self-taught in technology. They are not accustomed to calling customer service for help; instead, they ask the community on Yakker. While YakTrade does provide customer service, the call volumes are much lower than their competitors'. This allows them to focus additional resources on education, which is important to these new investors.

YakTrade clients wish to build high-quality portfolios that will grow over time, and YakTrade's strategy allows it to prosper along with its clients. High-quality, crowdsourced investment advice adds to the value of the social media platform and to YakTrade's overall product offering, retaining existing clients and attracting new ones. YakTrade will take social investing to the next level.

However, while YakTrade provides educational resources on a platform called Yakademy, the courses are rather dry and boring, and are underutilized by clients. In their initial analysis, Melissa and her team learned that confident, well-educated investors manage their portfolios more actively—driving commission revenues. But many YakTrade clients lack basic investment knowledge. Additionally, while many people share trading strategies on Yakker and some of the advice is excellent, much of the advice shared by clients is of low value, or even worse, it may be self-promotional or may encourage investors to pursue losing strategies. The result is that it's difficult for inexperienced investors to sort the wheat from the chaff. What YakTrade clients really need is insight into an investor's basis for knowledge and her long-term investment success.

Mike, director of client engagement solutions in the YakTrade IT department, has responsibility for the social media (Yakker), investor education (Yakademy), and service desk applications. Yakker has a vibrant community, but the challenge is that all of the voices have equal weight, and frankly, the people with less valuable information tend to share the most. The valuable advice provided by knowledgeable investors gets drowned out by the babble. Mike wants to give more weight to the voices that are providing more valuable advice. The challenge is to give the community tools to identify the people with the most valuable advice to share, raise the profile of those users, and make sure their voices are heard above the din.

As he sought solutions for these initial problems with the community, Mike at first dismissed the buzz around gamification as just the next fad. Then he attended a conference and sat in on a case study describing how gamification was used successfully to encourage employees to share knowledge using a collaboration tool at a large consulting firm. It seemed like a powerful technique that he could apply to the Yakker platform. A little more research led Mike to understand that gamification can also be used to engage people in training. Perhaps, he thought, they could gamify Yakker and Yakademy to take the YakTrade concept to the next level.

Gamification could help investors take the specific steps necessary to become more successful, and would allow them to demonstrate their achievements using badges or some other type of token. These symbols of achievement would enable the community to weigh in on the knowledge and success of the investor to determine the relative importance of the person's advice, simultaneously building the reputation of more knowledgeable and successful investors.

Mike discussed the opportunities for leveraging gamification with Tom Black, the executive vice president of investor services. At first Tom was skeptical about building games around people's financial portfolios. Mike explained that gamification isn't really about games, it's about engagement and motivation. Tom was still wary, but he understood that other organizations have had great success using gamification and agreed to explore the idea further.

Mike contacted Jessica at Kaleftic, the digital media agency that helped YakTrade with its social media site design and launch. He discovered that Kaleftic had recently completed a couple of gamification projects. Jessica thinks Mike's ideas can help Yak-Trade and its clients realize the true value of the platform.

As we've discussed, gamification is not about slapping points and badges onto an activity and expecting it to magically become more engaging. It is about understanding the players' goals and motivations and designing an experience that inspires them to achieve their goals. Tom and Mike both recognize the opportunity to provide more effective training and to crowd-source better advice from the community. But it's not going to be easy. Creating a gamified solution that engages people at an emotional level requires a deep understanding of the players. Their goals are not always rational or easy to identify, and they are not likely to be uniform across the target audience. What is needed is a process of discovery.

Gamified experience design must build solutions from the bottom up by employing a process called design thinking. Designers are empiricists by nature. They don't approach a problem with preconceived notions of the solution. They identify the underlying and sometimes hidden needs of the users as a basis for understanding what is required to solve the problem. Their approach is to collect a lot of information, look for relationships, and synthesize a solution.

Cory Eisentraut, the creative director on the Pain Squad application team, said, "We know that the best work comes out of getting inside of the problem and putting yourself in the place of the client or end user."

In fact, in the early design stages of Pain Squad, Cundari was thinking about calling the app "Gumshoe" and making the story about a private detective. But when they tested this concept with the kids, they found that none of the children had any idea what a gumshoe was. It forced them to rethink their approach and change the storyline to a police squad; and, of course, police forces have a built-in progression structure that was easily incorporated into the solution. As Cory recalled, "By striking out, it forced us to get to a much better place. That was a really big win for us."

APPLY DESIGN THINKING

When designers think about design, some of them are looking to solve problems that are much bigger than creating a sleek design for the next consumer gadget. These people are proponents of design thinking, which leverages the best approaches in design and applies them to myriad problems. According to one of design thinking's thought leaders, Tim Brown, president and

CEO of IDEO, "Design thinking is a human-centered approach to innovation that draws from the designer's tool kit to integrate the needs of people, the possibilities of technology, and the requirements for business success."[1]

The principles of design thinking can be applied to a broad range of problems and can augment conventional problem-solving approaches. Gamified experience designers should be wary of traditional software design approaches. In software development, one of the most common problem-solving approaches is decomposition.

Decomposition takes a big problem and breaks it down into much smaller individual problems that can be solved. It then aggregates the small solutions into a larger solution to address the larger problem. While this approach is appropriate for many complex software problems, it is not the best for designing gamified experiences. This approach addresses the obvious user requirements, but it typically doesn't consider user engagement and motivation. Software engineers rarely ask users what motivates them. Software is utilitarian, so the objective is to get something practical done, such as entering a sales order or scheduling an appointment. That is fine for software designed for utility and efficiency, but not for software designed for motivation. Without a deep understanding of the player's goals and motivations, typical software design approaches will likely result in a solution that meets specifications but fails to engage the audience.

According to IDEO, "Design thinking is a deeply human process that taps into abilities we all have but get overlooked by more conventional problem-solving practices. It relies on our ability to be intuitive, to recognize patterns, to construct ideas that are emotionally meaningful as well as functional, and to express ourselves through means beyond words or symbols."

Let's parse that statement to understand how design thinking applies to gamification. Design thinking is a "deeply human approach." Likewise, gamification must start with a player-centric approach. Designers of gamified solutions must start by exploring the goals and motivations of the players before considering how to deploy solutions. Second, design thinkers must be "intuitive to recognize patterns," and must do so by employing an empirical approach—exploring, collecting data, and recognizing relationship patterns to fully understand the nature of the problem to be solved. Third, design thinking is used to "construct ideas," and, as we will discover, gamified solutions are built over time, rather than taking a waterfall approach, in which design is finalized before development begins. Fourth, the solution must be "emotionally meaningful"—successful gamification solutions engage players at an emotional level. And finally, "express ourselves through means beyond words or symbols." Gamification uses words and symbols but leverages them to create meaningful experiences.

In the hands of a competent experience designer, the tools of gamification can be a powerful means of motivating people to achieve their goals. In this chapter, we will understand the player experience design process for gamification, incorporating the expertise of design thinkers.

STEP ONE: DEFINE THE BUSINESS OUTCOME AND SUCCESS METRICS

When they get started, Jessica asks Tom the first key question: What are YakTrade's business objectives in gamifying Yakker and Yakademy?

Tom replies that there are multiple objectives:

1. To empower clients with the knowledge to invest successfully
2. To crowdsource quality research from the client community
3. To increase commission revenues
4. To increase client growth and retention

But Jessica wants specifics. Exactly what graduation rate must Yakademy achieve to be considered a success? How will crowdsourced research quality be measured, and what are the targets? What is the target percentage increase in commission revenue per client? What are the client growth and retention targets? Tom needs to spend time consulting with some of YakTrade's senior managers to clearly articulate the business objectives.

Gamification is one of the newest shiny objects to emerge, and many organizations want to add it to their collection. I frequently have conversations with clients who want to implement a gamified solution—any solution, it doesn't matter what. They just want some gamification. Gamification is cool, and these clients are enamored with the trend rather than the business impact it will have. Gamification has itself become the objective. I generally ask these clients what business outcome they are trying to achieve, and that brings the conversation back to earth.

Having spent most of my career helping organizations evaluate disruptive trends and technologies for corporate deployment, I've learned that rule number one is: Do not invest in any trend or technology (including gamification) without first identifying the business outcomes you expect to achieve. Today, many people in organizations are enchanted with gamification itself and seem to be more focused on "doing something" than on achieving a clearly defined business outcome. This guarantees failure. One logical question highlights the concept: How can an organization achieve success without first defining what success is?

Once an organization defines the business need that gamification can address, the next step is to define the target outcomes and success metrics in sufficient detail. Many businesspeople describe business outcomes in vague terms such as "improving customer engagement" or "driving product innovation." But adding specifics will provide clearer direction, create a yardstick for success, and guide the limits of investment. Gamification is not the solution to all engagement problems, and having clearly defined business outcomes will help to determine whether it is suitable for the business challenge at hand.

The targeted business outcomes should be realistic, achievable, explicitly stated, and should include success metrics. For example:

- Increase website traffic by X percent in X months
- Increase customer testimonials by X percent in X months
- Increase member online purchase value by X percent in X months
- Increase new customer acquisitions by internal sales by X percent in X months
- Launch X innovation projects in X months
- Reduce average on-boarding duration to X days
- Increase course comprehension by X percent

In addition to identifying business outcomes, organizations need to understand the business disruptions that are driving the move toward gamification. Business disruptions are changes in the business environment, and are most often driven by factors external to the organization, such as customers migrating to new channels or competitors innovating at a faster rate. The underlying trend that is disrupting the business provides a context for the target business outcomes.

It's also important to test the alignment of the business outcome with the stated business strategies. What strategies does the initiative support that can be tied to the way business leaders will promote the idea?

STEP TWO: DEFINE THE TARGET AUDIENCE

Jessica recognizes the critical importance of getting to know the audience for Yakker's gamified solution. Yakker has more than five hundred thousand clients, so Jessica starts by asking for demographic information—age groupings, education level, gender, and family status. What is their clients' average net worth? Are they married or single? Do they own their houses and do they have mortgages? In many cases, the questions she asks cannot be answered with the data in the system, although Mike provides the Kaleftic project team with whatever information he can get from the existing system.

But it's not enough. So Jessica and her team hang out on Yakker. They Yak with clients from different geographical areas who are of varying ages and financial situations. They discover that only about 20 percent of the clients are active on Yakker, so they survey a group of clients to find out why more don't participate. They organize a client focus group that meets on Yakker to share ideas. The client community at YakTrade has some similarities but just as many differences. While they are mostly younger, the client base includes a sizeable share of older investors and a disproportionately high number of women. It includes independent business owners, professionals, and skilled workers. A lot of clients are parents (both single and married), so while most clients are saving for retirement, many are also saving for their children's education.

Jessica's team listens more than they talk. They wanted to find out what the clients value in Yakker and Yakademy, what they don't value, what prevents them from participating in the community, and what motivates them to join. They take extensive notes, and discover that there are common themes in what people are saying. This leads them to evolve a motivation map and goals for the engagement program. Eventually, they begin to characterize some of the common personality traits and motivations into "personas"—fictitious people who represent some of the common stories they are hearing from the clients.

It is critically important to define the target audience for any gamified solution. As mentioned in chapter 2, the target audience for gamified solutions, generally speaking, is customers, employees, or a community with a shared interest. Organizations have different core value exchanges with each of these audiences: customers typically exchange cash for a product or service; employees exchange their time and work for cash; and communities may exist to exchange information, build social networks, or work toward a shared goal, to name just a few. While each of these target audiences has some core value exchange, there are usually multiple and complex value exchanges happening at the same time. Gamification often addresses issues that are outside the core value exchange. In the Pain Squad example, the core value exchange between the hospital and the patients is providing treatment. The collection of pain data was outside of the core value exchange.

The intent in defining the target audience is to put boundaries around the people the organization needs to engage. This limits the number of different player types that need to be addressed with the solution, and therefore directs and guides design decisions. For example, in the Pain Squad case, the target audience was boys and girls between the ages of eight and eighteen who have been diagnosed with cancer. According to Dr. Stinson from SickKids, "That is a wide age range, and to find something that appealed to people in that age range for both boys and girls was difficult. Working through the storyboards with the kids really helped to make sure we were on the right track."

As we saw in earlier examples, the American Heart Association, Khan Academy, and Quirky all define their target audience as communities of interest—volunteers, students, and inventors, respectively. The DWP, DIRECTV, and NTT Data define their employees as their target audiences. Nike, Change Healthcare, and Barclaycard all define their customers as their target audiences. Having a clear understanding of the target audience can avoid misaligned player objectives that result in solutions that engage the wrong target audience, or simply fail to engage people at all.

The process of collecting information helps experience designers understand the demographics of the audience: gender, age group, income, location, and any other factors that may influence players' motivations. Of course, the demographics will never provide a homogeneous audience. Even in the tightest of demographic groups, there are individual variations of personality types, which need to be identified and categorized as well.

Explore the Target Audience

Once the target audience has been identified, expect to devote considerable time to learning about them. As we discussed, great designers build ideas from the bottom up by observing the audience, collecting data, and identifying relationships. Don't underestimate how important it is to spend time with the target audience. Talk to them, get to know them, learn what kind of people they are. Ask them what they like and what they dislike, as well as what works and what doesn't. If the target group is employees, ask them about their job and how they perform it. If the target group is customers, get to know what they value and what they don't. Ask them why they buy your company's product instead of the competitors' offerings. Ask them how the product or service experience can be improved.

Data collection will be guided by the business objectives, but should not be constrained by them. Use open questions. Be prepared to capture unexpected results. Listen and watch for hints of motivation that reflect the business objectives. As we will see later, player objectives are often aligned with business objectives, but they are stated differently. Like two sides of the same coin, business and player objectives may have different faces but often represent the same thing.

Organizations seldom design gamified solutions for a single demographic or personality type. Understanding the motivations of the target audience allows the designers to engage the largest possible audience. The more they understand the players' personalities, the more likely they are to appropriately define the players' motivations and objectives. Most target audiences won't be homogeneous, but specific and common characteristics will become apparent. To understand the commonalities, categorize the characteristics and create personas to represent them.

Create Player Personas

A persona is an imagined individual who represents some of the common character traits of a group of people. For example, when designing We365, Free The Children and TELUS created a persona called Hannah. She is a fifteen-year-old girl who cares about causes. She lives in an urban environment in Canada and is active on social media. Then the team asked the question, "What would Hannah want?" After Hannah, the We365 team branched off to create personas for boys and other people.

Creating personas helps to avoid abstract discussions about the goal being quick returns or long-term growth. Each group has different goals and motivations, but once fictitious characters have been created to represent them, it's easier to identify their different goals and motivations. It's also then possible to have more focused discussions about each persona.

When Jessica's team completes the YakTrade audience profile, they generate four personas:

Daniel is a single thirty-six-year-old architect with a high income who is saving for his retirement. His portfolio is largely made up of blue-chip stocks and U.S.-focused, exchange-traded funds. His approach to investing is analytical and long term. He doesn't "play" the market. In relative terms, his only real risk exposure is to the market itself. His portfolio is solid and performing well. He has logged onto Yakker and he did answer a few questions on portfolio balancing, but it didn't seem to be worth his time to share his advice. In his spare time, Daniel volunteers on a community planning council, using his expertise as an architect to turn vacant lots and buildings into recreational spaces in the more impoverished areas of the city.

Amanda is a thirty-eight-year-old schoolteacher, her husband is a radiologist, and they have two young children. Their combined income is comfortable, and they are saving for both their children's education and their retirement. Amanda looks after the household finances, but she doesn't really understand or trust the stock market. She looks to her parents for investment advice, and has the majority of her family's portfolio invested in low-risk bonds, but their portfolio is underperforming. Amanda checks into Yakker regularly and sees that other people are doing much better with their portfolios. She is beginning to feel she should shift some of her investments to equities, but she lacks the knowledge and confidence to change her portfolio.

Robert is a fifty-eight-year-old account executive in a software company. He is divorced, his kids are grown, and he has considerable disposable income. He sees the stock market as a game, and he is a player. He has just enough knowledge of the stock market to be dangerous. He thinks the stock market is an insider's game and that the key to success is being well connected. He is an active trader, always chasing the next rumor. Overall, his portfolio is losing money, but he knows that if he can just latch on to the next big thing, he will be wildly rich. He is very active on Yakker, where he is something of a rumor hub, collecting and disseminating the latest "insider scoop." Robert also finds the Yakker platform very useful in promoting the software company he works for and the products he sells in his day job. After all, he has stock options in the company and gets a commission on sales. Promoting the company and its products is a great side benefit of the platform. Some Yakker members criticize him for going off topic, but he's not worried. After all, any publicity is good publicity.

Sarah began her career catering parties twelve years ago, but that small business has grown to employ seventy people and now provides catering services for corporate cafeterias and hospitals. She is married with three children, and her stay-at-home husband manages the kids and the house. Over the years, supervising the baking of chickens and lasagna has lost its appeal, and Sarah has left most of the day-to-day management of the catering business to her operations director. The catering business has become her golden handcuffs. Her dream is to grow her portfolio until her investment income enables her to sell the catering business, so she can have more time with her family. Sarah has spent a lot of time and effort in developing her investment knowledge with Yakademy and other sources and it is paying off. Her investment portfolio regularly outperforms professionally managed funds. She follows about thirty companies closely, and she is quite active on Yakker. Her advice is highly valued and she has attracted a sizable following.

 With these definitions of the player personas, Jessica and the team know enough about the players to move forward with the project.

By creating the personas, Jessica and her team can consider that Sarah's goal is above-average portfolio growth using an active management and medium-risk strategy, while Daniel's goal is solid growth without the need to manage the portfolio on a daily basis. Amanda would like better performance on her portfolio but she lacks knowledge and confidence, while Robert is betting on the big win. At the end of this step, designers should have a list of personas, together with goals and motivations for each one.

STEP THREE: DEFINE PLAYER GOALS

Jessica's team now understands YakTrade clients' goals and motivations. While the team confirmed their expectations that all investors want to earn a decent return on their investments, they discovered that investment strategies are often misaligned with the client's goals in terms of risk tolerance and management. One of the big problems is a lack of knowledge, and another is that vocal community members like Robert have an outsized influence that leads many investors to make poor decisions. More of Daniel's advice would be welcome in the forum, and Daniel would likely contribute more if he were recognized for his contributions. Sarah provides very valuable information, but her signal is competing with those of people like Robert, who provide less valuable information. People like Amanda will benefit from being able to identify the quality of advice—from separating the Sarahs and the Roberts—that is being offered by Yakker members.

Jessica and her team also uncover unexpected client goals. For example, some clients promote stocks in companies they own or products and services of companies in which they have interests. Jessica discusses this unanticipated player goal with Tom and Mike, who are both aware that Yakker is being used for commercial purposes. While the platform was never intended for that purpose, they have been reluctant to shut down the clients who are advocating for their own companies. It's clear that promoting companies and services is not in the interests of the majority of YakTrade's clients, nor YakTrade itself, but censoring discussion is a sensitive issue. The ideal situation is to de-emphasize posts that are unrelated to investment.

Now the player goals are starting to take shape. It is clear that individual investors have different risk/return goals, they are

influenced by different sources, and there are some huge knowledge gaps.

In the end, the team defines four objectives for the players:

1. Developing basic investment knowledge
2. Highlighting knowledgeable investors for their contributions
   and successes
3. Having the tools to filter the signals from the noise
4. Using the platform to promote unrelated products and services

Jessica and the team feel good about these solution goals
since they are mostly aligned with both the player goals and the
business outcomes. Gamifying YakTrade now has an increased
probability of success.

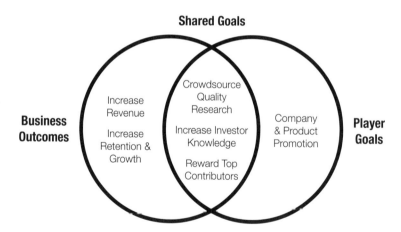

FIGURE 6–2: Defining Gamification Scope

Now it's time to analyze where business outcomes and player
goals overlap and where they don't. Not surprisingly, clients do
not deeply share YakTrade's goals to increase revenue, growth,
and retention. And Jessica's team has already established that
YakTrade doesn't support using the Yakker platform to promote
companies and products. That's okay; they can't really expect

all the goals to be aligned. Instead, it's important to focus on the overlap, the shared goals. Often, goals will be stated in different ways by the players and the organization. The area of overlap—the sweet spot for gamification—defines the opportunity space for engaging players to achieve their goals while at the same time achieving business goals.

WRAP UP

✓ It's important to use a process of discovery when designing a gamified experience. Gaining a deep understanding of both business and player goals enables the designer to compose the solution rather than decompose the problem. Typical software design approaches will likely result in a solution that meets specifications but fails to engage the audience.

✓ Clarity is critical in defining the business objectives. Designers must ensure the objectives are realistic, achievable, explicitly stated, and include metrics for success.

✓ Creating a gamified solution that engages people at an emotional level requires a deep understanding of the players. Their goals are not always rational, they may not be easy to identify, and they are not likely to be uniform across the target audience.

✓ Define the target audience, understand the demographics, and develop personas that represent the most typical personalities and goals of players.

✓ The area of overlap between defined business outcomes and discovered player goals is the sweet spot for gamification.

7
Designing a Gamified Solution

At their next status meeting, Jessica reviews the gamification solution goals with Tom and Mike. They are pleased with the way the project is progressing and suggest that, now that the goals are known, they start creating a series of contests to motivate clients to use Yakademy and to contribute more quality research to Yakker. Jessica doesn't agree with this approach. Rather than setting up a competitive environment using contests, she recommends creating a collaborative environment where everyone can benefit from improving the platforms.

As they discuss the matter further, Tom and Mike realize that defining the game structure is critical to the success of the solution. Not only do they need to consider how to get people to support other clients' contributions, they also need to take a position on the reward structure they are going to use, figure out how clients are expected to encourage one another, and determine how to maintain client engagement over a long period of time.

The motivation for participation must come from the clients themselves. Participants will be recognized for knowledge development, community contribution, and research quality. And the community will determine the quality of research. The YakTrade team will also use negative recognition from the community to diminish the use of the Yakker platform for company and product promotion.

STEP FOUR: DETERMINE THE PLAYER ENGAGEMENT MODEL

After defining the scope of the gamified solution and determining the players' goals and motivations, it's time to address decisions about how to structure the gamified solution. The player engagement model describes how the players will interact with the solution. In effect, it describes the way the solution is positioned.

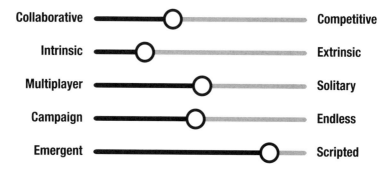

FIGURE 7–1: Player Engagement Model

Many people have preconceived ideas about what games are, and they make the mistake of applying their biases to the problem at hand. In fact, the engagement parameters of the solution are choices that need to be made, and each of these choices will have a huge impact on the way people interact with the solution and with other players. The challenge in gamification is to think through the implications of each of the game parameters and to make conscious choices about how the experience will be structured. Let's look at some of the most common parameters that need to be developed in the design phase:

Collaborative/Competitive. One of the basic parameters is the balance of competition and collaboration in the gamified experience. In this area, many people confuse games with gamification. The most common assumption is that games are competitive, and "a little competition never hurt anyone." This is the poker mind-set, where people conclude that every game is a competitive zero-sum game, just like poker. In many gamified solutions (but not all), this assumption is simply wrong. Games like poker are successful at driving a particular set of behaviors—a competitive, winner-takes-all mentality.

Sometimes players compete against one another and sometimes they compete against "the house." But in the majority of gamified solutions, there is no single winner and players are encouraging other players to be successful. Collaborative games are more likely to drive behaviors closely aligned with the solution objectives. For example, if the challenge is to train employees on company policies, the goal is not to have a winner, rather it is to train as many people as possible. Creating a competitive game structure is simply not appropriate in this case.

In collaborative gamified applications, players are rewarded for helping or encouraging other players to achieve their goals. As we saw in the Nike+ example, friends are invited to cheer the players on. Like most of these parameters, the level of competition and collaboration is a continuum, and there can be a combination of collaborative and competitive approaches. The most common way of combining collaboration and competition is to create team structures within the game. Players collaborate within the team, and teams compete with each other.

Intrinsic/Extrinsic. As we discussed earlier in the book, solutions in which players are primarily rewarded with tangible things are really rewards programs. Players are provided with a payback for doing something the organization wants. Gamified solutions rely primarily on intrinsic rewards, but that does not mean that extrinsic rewards have no place in gamified solutions. As we saw in the BBVA Game example, there can be a

combination of intrinsic and extrinsic rewards. BBVA customers are primarily motivated to use BBVA Game to learn how to
use web banking services. However, BBVA sweetened the deal
by offering some prizes, such as lotteries for tickets to sporting
events, as an additional incentive.

Multiplayer/Solitary. In card games, bridge has a very different
dynamic than solitaire. The difference is that in bridge, players
interact with one another while in solitaire players only interact
with the game. The same is true of gamification. In many gamified applications, the players interact only with the solution,
and there is no interaction between players, as we saw in the
Pain Squad example. In other gamified solutions there is a lot of
interaction between players; we saw this with the Quirky innovation solution. Gamified solution designers must determine at
the outset whether the solution will be designed to support mul-
tiplayer interactions or if game play will be between the player
and the game.

Campaign/Endless. By default, many people think that a gamified application should be endless, but often the objective is to
instill a new habit or learn a new skill, and these gamified applications should have a natural end. A good example is learning solutions; learning is endless but training in specific skills
are campaigns. Specific training courses have a natural end,
after the course is completed and the new skill is acquired. But
gamification of a learning management system is likely to be
positioned as an endless game, because training is an ongoing
activity in organizations.

Emergent/Scripted. As we discussed earlier, some gamified
applications are better suited to scripted game play while others
are better suited to emergent game play—emergent game play is
best where the outcome is unknown, as in innovation solutions.

With emergent solutions, designers focus more attention on the play space, creating the structure for emergent game play.

In situations where the outcome is known, scripted game play is a better choice. In both behavior change and training solutions, the outcome is known—we know what we want players to change or learn. In scripted solutions, designers focus most of their attention on the player journey.

STEP FIVE: DEFINE THE PLAY SPACE AND PLAN THE JOURNEY

Now that the objectives for the solution have been defined, Jessica's team starts to conceptualize what the solution will look like. They need to make decisions about the approach they will use, the platforms it will be delivered on, and how it will engage clients. As you will recall, the solution objectives are to:

1. Crowdsource quality research
2. Increase investor knowledge
3. Reward top contributors

Crowdsourcing quality research and rewarding top contributors are both behavior changes, and the play space to influence this behavior is the Yakker platform itself. The platform will be customized to enable players to recognize and reward top performers, and will include filters that help identify quality research. YakTrade already has considerable information on its clients—their individual holdings, portfolio performance, and the companies they are following. To protect client confidentiality, this information can be provided as a percentage of the overall portfolio without providing actual cash values. This information is currently private, but can be made public at the client's discretion. The team also decides to modify the client watch list to capture stock recommendations (buy, hold, sell) and target prices for the stocks they are holding and following. They will also extend the client profile to allow clients to describe their investment strategies and their primary decision tools for selecting investments (for example, technical chart analysis, sentiment indicators, stock valuation, analyst recommendations, or any other source). Also, information can be compiled across the entire client base to assess recommendations for different stocks. For example, if a thousand clients are following Google, Caterpillar, or Citigroup, the average recommendations and target price can be made available to investors.

Investors can search for people who have similar investment goals to determine who they should follow, based on their successes. People who follow another investor are notified when that investor makes a change in their holdings or recommendations. From a technical perspective, this is a simple change that would allow clients to optionally expose information that already exists.

Increasing investor knowledge is a skills development goal, and YakTrade already has the Yakademy platform, which provides video lessons on the basics of investing, but few people watch the videos. Tom and Mike couldn't understand why the course material was not being used. On previous projects, Jessica had learned that achievements were only valuable if they were hard to get. Passively watching a video was simply too easy. Now, the platform will be modified to structure the video lessons into a logical and progressive structure. For each video course, there will be a test of the content. Learners need to pass the test before moving on to the next video. While the tests ensure that the learner has understood the content, their real purpose is to confirm that the learner showed up. To take learning to the next level, the team will also build case study questions into the curriculum; these require essay answers to demonstrate a thorough understanding of the material. Other learners will be required to grade the answers of their peers to unlock grading on their own case study questions. In this way, peer review is used for quality control in learning achievements.

Designers of gamified applications must determine both the play space and the player journey. The play space may be a virtual place that exists only within a network of computers, as we saw in the Khan Academy example, or it can be a combination of virtual and real environments, like Nike+. The player journey is the path that you define for the players to take in the solution.

Play space. This is the environment that you provide for the players to engage with the game and with one another. In contrast to video games, most gamified solutions do not have elaborate virtual worlds with high-quality animation, simulations, and avatars. Most gamified solutions provide a very basic play space that can show players' profiles, progress, and all the tools necessary for the player to engage in the solution. For example, Khan Academy provides players with a profile, links to training videos ordered by topic, exercises to develop and test skills, and a space where teachers can see how students are progressing. There is not much that looks like a video game; this is not a criticism, it is simply to state that video game–like elements are not required to keep players engaged.

Innovation games often provide a rich set of tools for players to use. Quirky offers a space to submit ideas, vote on the ideas of others, and provide input for market research, product design, colors, materials, finishes, product name, and pricing. Because innovation solutions don't have a known outcome, the emphasis is on the play space rather than the player journey. In these solutions, the player journey is mostly focused on on-boarding activities, to get players familiar with the play space before turning them loose to innovate.

Player journey. This describes the path the players take through the solution. From on-boarding the players through taking them to advanced levels, designers must carefully balance challenge and skill as the player progresses, in order to maintain engagement.

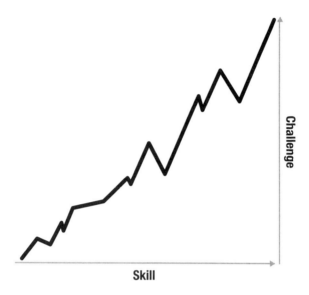

FIGURE 7–2: Player Journey

Gamified solutions are designed to present players with a series of actions or engagement loops that the players must master. Every attempt to complete the action is typically echoed with some kind of feedback (good or bad) to recognize the player's effort. These actions must be challenging for the player but must also be achievable given her skill level. Often, these actions are grouped together into missions or challenges that players must complete to earn a badge, move to the next level, or earn some other form of recognition.

STEP SIX: DEFINE THE GAME ECONOMY

Jessica's team starts to work out a system of points and rewards that will motivate the players to leverage the community and its resources and help them achieve their individual investment goals. Many of the achievements will relate to portfolio performance, so the motivation is already there; only the recognition is missing. But in other areas, clients need to be motivated to do things they haven't done before, such as recommending stocks or taking training. The team must be creative in defining rewards that are both challenging to achieve and highly valued by the players. One key to the solution is to leverage the knowledge of the top performers to make them visible across the community. To do this, they will use leaderboards of "sages" that show portfolio performance over different time periods. They will also show leaderboards of "beacons"—those who have the most followers. That way, a relative newbie like Amanda can quickly determine who she should follow to make better investment decisions.

While leaderboards recognize top performers, the team also needs to recognize the accomplishments of each player. Taking a lesson from the Boy Scouts and the Girl Scouts, they decide on badges as the primary rewards system. Recognizing that badges themselves have little value, they must ensure the rewards are meaningful to the players. The structure they put in place offers some easily achieved badges for early participation, to encourage members to get started. These include watching five videos and completing the test questions. But they increase the challenge level quickly so that the top-level badges are very difficult to achieve. This ensures a level of scarcity at the top levels that make these badges highly desirable (remember the skiing pin I tried for in the introduction to this book). Examples of higher challenge levels include master class badges for people who excel at case studies.

While strong portfolio performance is a kind of badge in its own right, the team decides to call out exceptional portfolio performance with badges like "Top Gun" for clients who achieved portfolio growth in the top 10 percent of the community over a single year; "Long Tail" for clients who are successful in selecting small-cap stocks that outperform; and the coveted "Pro" badge for portfolios that outperformed the S&P 500 over five years.

To encourage people to make recommendations, the team creates on-boarding badges for people who follow ten, twenty, or thirty companies. In the future, recommendations will be ranked against performance to reward client achievements in accurately predicting winners.

Games, rewards programs, and gamification solutions all have an in-game economy, although it typically is not an economy based on money. The in-game economy is composed of the incentives and rewards that the players are awarded for successfully performing tasks, completing challenges, or achieving goals. It is critical to understand player objectives and motivations to create a game economy that implements a player-centric design. As I discussed in chapter 1, video games are more likely to use intangible rewards that amuse the players to engage them. Rewards programs are a value exchange in which players are given mostly tangible rewards for performing tasks that the organization values. As we now know, one of the key distinctions of a gamified application is the calculated use of intrinsic rewards to create a meaningful experience for the players.

There are four basic currencies that players accumulate in game economies—fun, things, social capital, and self-esteem— and these are implemented through game mechanics such as points, badges, and leaderboards. These game mechanics are simply tokens of different currencies of motivation that are being applied to reward players.

- Fun is the primary currency of games.
- Things are the primary currency of rewards programs.
- Self-esteem and social capital are the primary rewards of gamified solutions.

It's important to look at these as guidelines rather than rigid criteria. Games certainly use self-esteem and social capital as part of their game economies—players increase in levels, powers, and recognition throughout the game. Rewards programs also use self-esteem—remember that the really important reward for Ryan Bingham in *Up in the Air* was to get his name on the side of a plane. Also, BBVA used prizes (things) as a reward in their gamified solution, as does Samsung Nation. It's better to be a pragmatist rather than a purist. Sometimes players need tangible rewards to engage in some tasks that hold no intrinsic value for them. Additionally, some of the purely fun aspects of games can create a more engaging experience for the players. Player goals and motivations will naturally guide designers to leverage self-esteem and social capital types of rewards, but designers should also be open to using other rewards to engage players when necessary.

FIGURE 7–3: Game Economy

Fun. Although seldom used in gamified applications, in video games simple elements of fun make up a large part of the game economy. Video games have a constant barrage of lights and sounds that make playing the game an exciting experience. Advanced graphics and story lines make players feel like they are saving the world or winning a battle. As we saw in the Pain Squad example, a story line featuring a police squad was used to drive motivation. These are important elements of game design. Most fun game mechanics have a fleeting impact in the game economy—they are not often durable nor do they offer tangible rewards. In gamified applications, the most common use of fun is through surprise rewards—unexpected, random rewards that engage players with a feeling that they are never certain what will happen next. We saw an example of this earlier with NTT Data's training programs, which used surprise trivia questions from senior managers to encourage people to check in to the system regularly.

Things. This currency includes the tangible items that can be collected and sometimes exchanged within the solution. These are often implemented as points that can be redeemed for cash or rewards. Tangible rewards are really the domain of rewards programs, but are sometimes used in gamified applications when the desired behavior is not aligned with a player's goals. But all too often experience designers lack either creativity or a clear understanding of player goals and motivations, and thus must rely on "things" to keep players engaged. As we know, most rewards programs rely on tangible rewards as the basic tokens of currency in their economies.

Self-esteem. As we have learned from author Dan Pink, autonomy, mastery, and purpose are the primary intrinsic motivators, and gamified applications use a number of different game mechanics to recognize accomplishments. Games and gamified applications provide players with challenges, give constant feedback on progression, and recognize achievements with praise, leveling up, access to exclusive services, or badges of achievement. All of these rewards work to build the player's self-esteem and maintain engagement in the game.

Social capital. People are motivated when others within their social circles recognize their achievements. Designers of gamified applications can motivate players with recognition as a reward within the gamified application. The social circle often includes other players in the game when player interaction is built into the solution. It can also be extended to external social networks such as Twitter, Facebook, or LinkedIn, to increase the impact of the recognition in social circles. For example, gamified applications can link to Facebook to post achievements on a user's wall (with permission), like the Vail EpicMix application does. Social capital is a powerful motivator, and includes rewards like status, peer recognition for player contributions, or other achievements by the player.

Amplifying Motivation with Social Media

By gamifying YakTrade, Jessica and the Kaleftic team leveraged the Yakker platform far beyond its original purpose to make it a platform for engaging clients in a journey to more successful investing. Yakker is much more than a place to discuss investments, it has become a platform for identifying which members of the community are making the best investment choices and providing the highest value contributions. By adding dynamic rewards and recognition it becomes more engaging, so that even people like Daniel are motivated to share their investment strategies. It also achieved the desired effect of de-emphasizing the bad advice and rumors that people like Robert contribute to the community. By leveraging reputation, Robert and folks like him diminish in influence—they are no longer hubs disseminating bad advice, rather they become lonely voices that most people pay little attention to. Top performers are the rock stars of the community and provide valuable advice to less knowledgeable clients.

Humans are social animals. From the day we are born, we are dependent on family and friends for our growth and success, and indeed for our very survival. As social animals, we collaborate and compete within our networks to develop skills, achieve career goals, and even to select a partner. We are profoundly impacted by and dependent upon our social networks, but the nature of our social networks has forever changed. No longer are we limited by physical contact to a circle of friends in our towns, schools, workplaces, places of worship, or clubs. Today, we can maintain a larger circle of friends through regular virtual contacts using social media.

Killer apps have always focused on connecting people, and with more than one billion users, Facebook has forever changed the way people interact and engage. As a platform for engagement, Facebook provides an unparalleled opportunity to connect and share information with the friends who are most important to us. While Facebook is the most prominent, there are many other social networks that we connect to, such as professional networks (e.g., LinkedIn) and enterprise social networks (e.g., Yammer), that also play an important role in our overall social network profile.

Social networks provide a window into our personalities, a place where we can share our comments, photos, articles— anything we feel may be interesting to our network of friends. The online personality we create has a huge impact on the way our friends see us. Facebook users will recognize the feeling of surprise you get when you learn that your cousin is an opera aficionado or your old high school buddy is taking flying lessons. Who knew they had it in them? In fact, social recognition of our achievements is a powerful motivator. As both gamification and social networks engage people primarily on an emotional level, there are clear and complementary links between them.

Increasingly, people are sharing their achievements on social networks. LinkedIn has recently added certifications, honors and awards, and publications, among other accomplishments, to help members build their personal brand. Social networks offer a virtual means similar to placing a degree on your office wall or a trophy on your shelf. They are a megaphone for your achievements that is not limited to physical space. Gamified solutions often enable users to post their achievements on social network sites, allowing them to boost their personal brands. As Paul Wilmore of Barclaycard noted "When people get to the higher levels of status, you actually get other community members congratulating them."

STEP SEVEN: PLAY TEST AND ITERATE

Jessica and the Kaleftic team realize they are unlikely to get everything right in theory, so they engage a focus group in play testing the solution. As they develop the early storyboards for the new Yakker and Yakademy applications, they test them with the focus group to get their feedback. Once the gamified features have been incorporated into the solutions, they roll out first to the focus group, incorporate their feedback, and then have a limited rollout to 5 percent of the client audience. By capturing data around all of the client interactions in the engagement loops, they are able to see what works and what doesn't, and tune the game mechanics before the final rollout. Tuning continues after the launch, incorporating changes based on client feedback and adding additional features. Because the solution is intended to drive long-term engagement, there will be periodic updates, with new challenges and achievements to ensure that players stay engaged over time.

Video games have a development approach that can take years and cost millions of dollars, moving in stages from the initial idea, to funding and preparing for production, to actually producing the video game, and finally to marketing and distribution. The video game is launched with much fanfare. If initial sales are good, the game may be a success, and all of the time, effort, and money pays off. Developing a video game is a long-term, high-risk, and high-cost endeavor.

Often, people start a gamification initiative with the preconceived idea that it is like creating a video game. That there will be a long development cycle and a finished product will be rolled out. Actually, gamification doesn't usually work that way. Unlike console video games, with gamification, the product is never final. It will continue to evolve long after the launch. In fact, the initial launch of a gamified solution should include just enough features to engage the audience and meet the business objectives.

Gamified solutions should evolve over time to add new functionality, to engage the audience in new ways, and to keep it fresh. From the first day of the launch, you will start to learn a great deal about the audience and how they interact with the solution. This knowledge will guide the evolution of the solution over time.

While we have examined a lot of theory on motivation, in practice it is hard to predict what will motivate people. Designing a great gamified application in theory and having great success are two very different things. While the approach I have described here will help to avoid some of the major pitfalls in designing a gamified application, do not expect to get it 100 percent right the first time around. Gamification solutions are developed iteratively. Use a pilot group of players who can test the solution and provide feedback throughout the design/development phases. Early concepts can be tested with storyboards, as we saw in the Pain Squad example.

In cases where the solution is targeted at a very large audience, an incremental launch that exposes the solution to a small percentage of the audience will allow for additional tuning before the solution is made available to the broader audience.

Collect data on all player interactions with the solution. Once the solution has been released, this data will be invaluable in determining which engagement cycles are working, and which are not. This will enable you to tune the application over time, modifying those aspects of the solution that are not engaging to the players.

WRAP UP

✓ The player engagement model directs how players will interact with both the solution and other players. It also determines the reward structure and engagement cycle.

✓ Most gamified solutions don't resemble game worlds, rather they are implemented as a layer of game mechanics on top of an activity that is often played out in the real world.

✓ The player journey presents players with a series of actions or engagement loops they must master to proceed through the solution.

✓ The game economy must be aligned with player objectives and motivations to provide the rewards—fun, things, social capital, or self-esteem—to players for successfully performing tasks, completing challenges, or achieving goals.

✓ Social media integration enables the recognition of player achievements by peer networks and is a powerful amplifier of motivation.

✓ Unlike video games, gamified solutions should evolve over time to add new functionality, to engage the audience in new ways, and to keep them fresh.

8
Common Design Pitfalls

I recently had a conversation with a software vendor client who wanted to gamify the company's software offering. His opening statement was, "we just need to add some points and badges, which seems easy." His perspective is quite typical of many people—that gamification is technically a very easy problem to solve—and they are right. But as you now understand, the challenge of gamification is designing the player experience, not the technology. Many organizations proceed without clearly understanding the nature of the challenge, and many of them will fail. Gamified solutions fail for three primary reasons:

1. The business outcomes haven't been clearly defined.
2. The gamified solution has been designed to achieve the organizational goals rather than the player goals.
3. The solution engages people on a transactional level rather than an emotional level.

Having gotten this far in the book, you appreciate these larger issues, so we won't dwell on them any more here. In this chapter, let's explore some of the less common but still important pitfalls to avoid when developing gamified solutions.

FAILING TO MANAGE THE GAME ECONOMY

The same forces that apply to real economies also apply to game economies. All games have economies, and the points, badges, and awards used in gamification have an intrinsic value. Designers of gamified applications determine the "money supply" in the game economy. If they flood the game with easily achieved badges, they will devalue the badges for the people who already hold them. If they increase the point levels required to attain achievements, they introduce price inflation. In gamified solutions, unredeemed points are unrealized value by the players and can create an imbalanced game economy. Players should be motivated to use points to realize value.

Designers of gamification solutions need to be aware of their impact on the players should they make changes to the game economy. One of gamification's fundamental attractions is that it provides transparency. It's demotivating to make any change that has a negative impact on the players. Players know what rewards they can expect for the effort they invest. Tinkering with the game economy damages trust, which in turn damages engagement. While you don't need to be an economist to manage a game economy, you do need to be aware of the impact you are having when you make changes to the game economy.

JUMPING TO THE ENDGAME

People love shortcuts. Who can blame them? Why go through the hard work of really understanding player motivations and goals when you can simply prod people to action with free stuff like badges? I have almost daily conversations with clients who have heard the hype around gamification and have come to the conclusion that it is quick, easy, and effective. All they need to do is add some badges to get people to do what they want. They are missing the middle. Jumping from what the organization wants to how to reward people for doing it misses the whole point of gamification. This is just a fast path to failure.

As we have learned in the previous chapters, successful gamification is a process. It involves the time-consuming work of gaining a real understanding of the target audience and their motivations and goals. There's no way to gather this knowledge without taking the time to understand the players. You could guess, but then you would just be guessing.

Google guessed and apparently guessed wrong. In July 2011, Google introduced "Google News Badges." The idea was to engage readers of Google News by showing them "how voracious a news reader you are by earning Google News badges as you read articles about your favorite topics. The more you read, the higher level badge you'll receive, starting with Bronze, then moving up the ladder to Silver, Gold, Platinum, and finally, Ultimate."[1] Google offered more than five hundred badges to cover different topics and different levels, and the badges could be shared with friends to "Tell them about your news interests, display your expertise, start a conversation, or just plain brag about how well-read you are."

Unfortunately, this particular project seemed doomed from the start. It was unclear why people would value these badges. It didn't appear to align with people's motivations or to signify the achievement of any meaningful goal. Perhaps Google came to the same conclusion. Google announced it would discontinue Google News Badges just fifteen months later.[2]

The Medal of Honor is the highest military honor bestowed on U.S. military personnel, and it is awarded by the president of the United States for personal acts of valor, above and beyond the call of duty. But it too is just another badge. Points, badges, and levels are some of the many game mechanics that are used in gamification, but they represent progress and achievement. They are not the achievement itself. They are simply signposts on the journey to mastery. One of the pitfalls in gamification is the tendency to focus on the points, badges, and leaderboards rather than the meaningful achievements they represent.

BEING INAPPROPRIATELY COMPETITIVE

As we discussed in the previous chapter, most gamified solutions are best positioned using collaborative engagement models rather than competitive ones. As many people consider gamification to be an extension of games, the misconception that gamification is competitive is widespread. As we discovered in chapter 1, the primary objective in gamification is to motivate people—generally, the broadest audience possible. In contrast, the primary objective in games is to entertain or amuse people. In head-to-head games, there is almost always a clear winner. In gamification, we most often want everyone to win. This is clearly true in gamified training solutions that are trying to help everyone learn. And it is usually true in behavior change solutions that are encouraging everyone to adopt the new behavior.

There are some exceptions where hybrid competitive/collaborative structures can be effective, most often in innovation solutions. The most common is where the players are formed into teams, and they collaborate within their teams but compete against other teams. This structure is useful because it creates peer pressure for each individual to perform within the team. Innovation solutions are the exception in gamification, the one in which competitive games produce the desired results. Often in innovation solutions, the objective is to select the single "best" solution and there is only one winner, so competitive games are appropriate.

Let's examine one case where direct competition is appropriate in gamification. The U.S. Defense Advanced Research Projects Agency (DARPA) has used contests (called grand challenges) to develop new technologies for many years. The winners of these challenges are rewarded with a cash prize and, more importantly, the prestige that goes along with victory. As I am writing this book,

DARPA is running a robotics challenge, "to generate groundbreaking research and development so that future robotics can perform the most hazardous activities in future disaster response operations, in tandem with their human counterparts, in order to reduce casualties, avoid further destruction, and save lives."[3] The teams come from the most prestigious universities, NASA, and defense companies. The prize for the winning team is $2 million. Since the goal of DARPA is to develop advanced technologies and select a single "best" solution, using a competitive game structure is appropriate.

While contests and other competitive games can be appropriate for some problems, there are many solutions where they are inappropriate but still commonly used. Competitive games can be highly engaging for the top performers, but may be uninteresting or even demotivating for all but those select few. This is often the case with sales contests, where the top-performing salesperson is awarded a trip to some exotic locale. This structure can create intense competition for the already high-performing top tier of salespeople, but it does very little to move the middle and bottom tiers of salespeople, where there is a greater opportunity to increase overall revenue.

CREATING SKILL/CHALLENGE IMBALANCES

Angry Birds is simple. Players are presented with a bird, preloaded in a slingshot. The only thing to do is pull back on the bird and let it go. The bird flies through the air and a pile of stuff comes into view, and if you are lucky enough to hit the target on the first launch, some of the stuff falls down and points flash up on the screen. On the second pull of the slingshot, you discover you can aim. Congratulations, you have learned to play Angry Birds.

Angry Birds, like most great video games, does not require players to read extensive manuals to get started. Video games can become extremely complex, but the challenge builds over time. Players are taught to play by being presented with obvious things to do. Creating a simple on-boarding experience is one of the things that video games really excel at, and one thing that designers of gamified solutions can learn from.

One of the common challenges in gamified solutions is that learning to play is often hard, and sustaining engagement is difficult. Players should learn how to engage the solution within the solution itself. The first steps should be obvious, and early achievements should be very easy to reach. Players need to feel they are accomplishing something right away.

In Duolingo, English-speaking players learning Spanish are presented with phrases to complete like, "Soy un/una hombre." The player starts by having to choose the correct article—you've got a fifty–fifty chance. If you guessed "una" you would be wrong, but it's quite easy to deduce that "un" is correct. Congratulations, you've learned something right away. Get it right, win some points!

Sustaining engagement requires balancing skill and challenge over time. In Duolingo, like many of the examples we have seen, the solutions become quite complex over time and continue to challenge even the most advanced players. But they are great examples of easing people gently into the solution before adding challenge and complexity as players develop their skills. Remember, designers of gamified solutions need to carefully balance skill and challenge as players advance through the solution. Mihály Csíkszentmihályi, a researcher on positive psychology, described the state of a person who is fully engaged in an activity that balances skill and challenge as achieving a state of "flow."[4]

TARGETING THE WRONG AUDIENCE

One problem that sometimes arises in gamified solutions is targeting the wrong audience with imagery and rewards. If your audience is romance novel readers, giving away tickets for wrestling matches or monster truck racing is likely not the best way to reward them. Your energy-reduction solution should probably not be adorned with cute, fuzzy bears. Using racehorses to represent employees in a performance management solution is likely to send the wrong message. Anything that looks like FarmVille is probably going to miss the mark.

There could be many reasons for these mismatches between the gamified solution and the target audience. The most common reasons are:

Not knowing the target audience. Without clarity around the player personas you are targeting, it is easy to misalign the context and reward structure for a gamified application.

Attracting an audience, any audience. Many organizations use metrics like the number of unique visitors and activities on the website as key indicators of engagement. These metrics are not useful if the audience you are attracting is not the audience who buys your products. In some cases, it seems that gamification solutions are designed to simply attract any audience at all.

Building a game that *you* would like. Sometimes gamified solutions do not appear to be aligned with their target audience, rather they seem to have been designed to attract people like the team that built them. It's easy to fall into the trap of building a game that you would like and losing site of the target audience.

Of course, the solution to misaligned audience issues is straightforward. You need to develop a deep understanding of the target audience demographics, motivations, and goals, and design solutions that will engage them.

MANDATING MOTIVATION

Gamification solutions are most likely to be successful when players opt in to use the system. Regardless of the quality of the gamified solution, it's unlikely to have the voluntary participation of 100 percent of the target audience. Some people are simply not going to engage. While this is not a problem for the majority of gamified solutions, in some cases it can be problematic.

Opt-in participation is particularly challenging in employee-facing solutions where participation is sometimes imposed by managerial decree rather than by employee choice. The types of solutions most often affected include training, change management, and performance management solutions where employee participation is sometimes mandatory.

Recent studies have shown that consent is a key factor in the success of gamified solutions. In a field study to determine the impact of consent on a performance management solution, the researchers concluded, "In our field experiment, we find that games, when consented to, increase positive affect at work, but, when consent is lacking, decrease positive affect and performance."[5]

Ideally, gamified solutions should not be forced upon the target audience; rather, users should be provided the opportunity to opt in to the solution. Mandatory participation can lead to negative results, and may cause at least part of the audience to either ignore the solution or have a negative reaction to participating.

ADDING WORK TO THE WORK

Often, gamification is implemented as a game layer on top of an existing process. To the extent possible, the game mechanics should be transparently integrated into the solution that supports the process rather than implemented as a separate solution. This is particularly important in employee-facing solutions. For example, if the gamified solution is focused on encouraging salespeople to enter contact information into the CRM solution, the game mechanics that track the entering of contact information must be built into the CRM solution, and not implemented as a separate solution that requires salespeople to duplicate the effort in both the CRM solution and a separate gamified solution. By integrating the capture of the desired actions into the existing systems, there is no additional work on the part of the players to have their activities counted. Creating stand-alone gamification solutions when the activities are already supported by another solution adds work to the work, and players will quickly resent it, causing them to disengage.

GAMING THE SYSTEM

Bernie Madoff, a Wall Street stockbroker and chairman of his own investment firm, ran a Ponzi scheme that duped thousands of investors out of billions of dollars over a couple of decades until he was finally caught in 2008. It was the largest financial fraud in U.S. history. A Ponzi scheme doesn't make money from investments; rather, it uses the capital from new investors to return profits to existing investors. This type of scam was named after Charles Ponzi, who ran such a scheme in the 1920s, but this type of scheme has been around since the eighteenth century. Clearly, there are rules to prevent this type of scheme, but Bernie Madoff found the loopholes that allowed him to game the system. A Ponzi scheme needs a few essential ingredients to work: trusting investors, a compliant auditing firm, and sleepy regulators. A Ponzi scheme is a form of gaming the system— getting around the rules to achieve a goal—in this case, making a lot of money. Bernie Madoff made off with about $18 billion until caught, and sentenced to 150 years in prison.

"The greater the risk, the greater the reward" is a common

expression to describe the risk/reward profile of investments. In gamification, the converse is true: the greater the reward, the greater the risk—the risk that someone will try to game the system. One of the risks of gamification is that winning the game becomes the player goal, rather than playing the game. When winning becomes the objective, some players will look for a loophole in the solution that allows them to progress and achieve goals without performing the activities that are defined in the solution. Clearly, this leads to unintended consequences. The more closely the solution objectives align with the player objective, the less likely it is that players will look for loopholes and shortcuts to achieving the goals.

While the rewards of stealing money from investors are great, the rewards for gaming a gamified solution are not nearly as significant. But if players find chinks in the armor of the system, they will take advantage of them. For example, Digg, a social news website, was a victim of its own community. In 2005, a user who went by the name of KoolAidGuy had discovered how to promote stories to the front page by taking advantage of a flaw in the system. He (or she) used it to promote articles to the front page, and exposed the flaw publically.[6] Not surprisingly, faithful Digg users were upset. One user posted, "Everyone who reads Digg knows of a user who calls himself KoolAidGuy. In short, this user started by showing the Digg community an error in the system, however, long after the problem became apparent, he continues to spam Digg, completely destroying its value."[7]

The lesson learned is that even when there is no money at stake, people can find chinks in the system and exploit them, simply because they can. To mitigate the risk, gamification designers need to think like a hacker and work to analyze the structure and rules of the solution to try to find the loopholes before players do.

WRAP UP

✓ Players value and rely on the game economy and expect it to remain a level playing field. Apply caution when adjusting it or you may damage trust, which, in turn, damages engagement.

✓ Successful gamification is a process of composing an engaging experience for a target audience. Plan to spend considerable time gaining a real understanding of the players and their motivations and goals.

✓ One of the traps in gamification is the tendency to focus on the points, badges, and leaderboards rather than the meaningful achievements they represent.

✓ Use competition judiciously, as it is often not aligned with the business objectives and can reduce motivation of underachieving players.

✓ To sustain player engagement, create an easy on-boarding experience and then balance skill and challenge over time.

✓ Gamification solutions are most likely to be successful when players opt in to use the system.

✓ One risk of gamification is that winning the game may become the player goal, rather than playing the game. Then, players may look for loopholes to game the system.

9

Managing for Success

Gamification projects must be proposed, funded, and managed just like any other change initiative. The broader topic of managing change projects is outside the scope of this book, and there are many other excellent resources on the topic. For now, let's focus on the areas where gamification projects differ from other change initiatives. The most important difference in gamification projects is in the design approach, and the specifics will be explored in this chapter.

SELLING GAMIFICATION TO BUSINESS LEADERS

Gamification is an unfortunate word. Perhaps it would be better to call it "motivication," but that would also be another silly word. The real problem is how the majority of people understand gamification. As we discussed earlier, gamification and games do share some of the same game mechanics, like points, badges, and leaderboards, but the relationship between games and gamification ends there. Gamification is about motivation, not fun. But the distinction is lost on many people, and it makes gamification a hard sell.

Given the fact that there is so much written on gamification that makes statements like, "gamification turns work into fun," it is easy to understand how businesspeople may react. Many business leaders see themselves as overseers of serious organizations;

they don't do fun. They are quite proud of that, and they are certainly not going to change because of the latest trend. If you are attempting to initiate a gamification project, you may need to adjust stakeholders' perspectives on gamification before they will even consider investing in it.

Dispel the myth that gamification is about fun. If you can convince senior management that gamification is really about motivating customers, employees, and communities of interest, you are on your way to convincing them of the benefits.

The early adopters of gamification took a leap of faith that the projects they were investing in would have some return. I applaud their faith. Many of these people were true believers and were prepared to take the risk of investing money without an established track record of return on those investments. You are probably not going to be so lucky.

The majority of business leaders are risk averse. They do not want to be first movers; rather, they want to be fast followers. They will look for proven examples of how gamification can achieve business outcomes. Many of the early case studies on gamification focused on what organizations are doing and did not include the business results that were achieved. In this book, I have highlighted some successful gamification solutions, and every day more successful cases are appearing in Gartner research, at gamification conferences, and in the media. It's necessary to collect case study examples of successes in other organizations to convince management that those successes can be replicated in your company. A reasonably solid business case to justify the investment will be required for most gamification initiatives in the future.

GAMIFICATION PROJECT ROLES AND SKILLS

Most IT solutions are focused on increasing the efficiency and/ or effectiveness of business processes. A gamified solution is qualitatively different. A gamified solution is primarily designed to engage and motivate users. Unsurprisingly, a gamification project is unlike most other IT projects, and it requires many different skills to be successful.

Gamification solutions are inevitably delivered using software, but they require a wide range of skills beyond the traditional proficiencies of software developers. People like digital strategists, behavioral psychologists, experience designers, and marketing specialists should also be part of the team. Depending on the use (to change behaviors, develop skills, or drive innovation), there may be other specialists' knowledge required, including the expertise of innovation specialists, educators, trainers, or coaches. Specific subject matter expertise will also be required on the topic that is being addressed. For example, in the YakTrade project we described earlier, specialists with knowledge of investing and finance would be required. The end users must also be represented, usually in focus or pilot groups.

Gamification project core teams are generally quite small (often fewer than ten people committed full time) but the broader project team will include many people with specialized skills who are working on the project on a part-time basis. Compared with other change projects, gamification solutions tend to be quite small both in terms of resources and cost. But gamification solutions are not free. They require resources and planning like any other project. Because they are small, they are sometimes not taken seriously in organizations and they suffer from "hobby project" status. These projects often have an outsized impact on the organization, and need to be accorded status aligned with the business impact rather than the project size.

The leader of the business unit most closely aligned with the target audience will likely be the sponsor for any gamification initiative. If the target audience is customers, the chief marketing officer is a likely candidate, and if the target audience is employees and the application is training, the vice president of human resources or the director of training are the likely sponsors. Except in cases where the gamified solution is specifically focused on the IT department, IT should play a supporting role in gamification solution development, with the business unit sponsor taking the lead.

The information technology (IT) department will be involved, particularly if the solution needs to integrate with corporate solutions. For example, the BBVA development team needed to work with the corporate web banking and security teams to enable integration with web banking services. Even if the solution stands alone and does not require integration with any corporate systems, it is advisable to liaise with the IT group, as they can add value in selecting the technology architecture, negotiating contracts with external service providers, and supporting the application over time.

SELECTING A TECHNICAL APPROACH

Gamification platforms and vendors provide a full suite of tools and services to accelerate your gamification projects. Basically, there are three approaches to developing a gamification solution: custom development, purpose-built solutions, and generalized gamification platforms.

Custom development. This approach provides the greatest flexibility, but may not be the most cost effective. As the name implies, the gamified solution is designed, developed, and deployed using internal and/or external resources. Organizations that have an internal IT organization may want to leverage these resources to develop a gamified solution. For these organizations, there are a couple of points to consider.

Typical IT development teams often do not have any experience in developing gamified solutions. They often have the technical skills (gamified solutions do not tend to be technically complex), but they lack the skills to understand how to engage and motivate people. Standard development skills sets need to be augmented with people who understand experience design.

Often, the analytics are overlooked by internal IT development teams. As we will see, gamified solutions typically evolve over time as the solution is tuned to optimize the player experience. This requires the collection and analytics of player interaction, and this needs to be addressed from the outset of technical design work.

These risks can be mitigated to some extent by leveraging the experience of a growing number of organizations that offer custom gamification solutions development. These organizations have experience developing gamified solutions and can leverage their knowledge of experience design and analytics. Custom gamification solutions development practices are being built within the larger, traditional outsourced development service providers, but there is also a fast-growing number of boutique service providers. These smaller providers often evolve from delivering advertising and digital media services to delivering gamification solutions. Some examples profiled in this book include Cundari, an advertising and branding agency that developed Pain Squad, and the now defunct Natron Baxter, which developed HeartChase for the American Heart Association and had a portfolio of custom-built gamified solutions for a variety of clients.

Purpose-built solutions. A growing number of purpose-built solutions is appearing on the market. Most prominent of these are horizontal solutions that address a growing number of areas such as innovation management, call centers, and customer relationship management. There is also a growing number of vertically focused solutions such as financial services training, restaurant/food services, and health care. Purpose-built solutions have the advantage of being tested in the market, therefore reducing the risks of failure, and they are also likely to be lower in cost than custom-developed solutions. On the downside, they will not provide long-term competitive advantage, as these same solutions are available to competitors as well. Organizations that are planning to deploy a gamified solution should evaluate the market to determine if there is a proven solution available that addresses the business challenge.

Generalized gamification platforms. These platforms support the integration of game mechanics and player analytics into solutions that have many different uses. A small number of generalized gamification platforms and vendors are available to support the design and implementation of a wide variety of gamified solutions. Gamification platforms provide general-purpose gamification tools, such as game mechanics and player analytics that can be integrated into a wide variety of solutions on many computing platforms.

Because these gamification platforms have been mainly exploited in consumer-facing solutions, vendors have the most experience in this area and with platforms that are tuned for this market. As gamification begins to be more broadly deployed in other business areas, vendors have begun to offer solutions and services that can support the gamification of internally focused business functions within organizations. Generalized gamification platforms are typically delivered as software as a service (SaaS) and provide:

• Game mechanics and rewards: Using APIs, these services provide the core game mechanics such as points, badges, leaderboards, and quests. End-user organizations can leverage these services to engage users and lead them through the player journey.

• Management tools: These enable end-user organizations to manage user registration and other administrative tools, as well as aspects of gamification integration.

• Social media integration or services: These provide linkages to popular social media sites such as Facebook and/or may manage a social network or other communities within the gamified solution.

• Analytics: The collection and analysis of user actions is needed to enable gamified solution designers to understand the aspects of the game that users find engaging—and which ones they do not find engaging—to enable tuning of the solution. Analytics also provides a mechanism to determine whether the gamified solution is meeting business objectives.

Leveraging the gamification platforms provided by vendors can significantly reduce development time, costs, and risks by using a specialized set of vendor tools. Costs can be minimized when organizations embarking on a gamification initiative use the vendor's infrastructure in the cloud, which is particularly important for solutions with unknown or highly variable demand, because services are provided in an elastic cloud model. By far, the greatest risk in gamification is poorly designed solutions, and the largest barrier to success is the lack of gamification design skills within organizations. Besides offering technologies that support gamification, these platform vendors also provide consultants with experience in designing and developing gamified solutions. In some cases, they also offer specialized skills in areas such as behavioral science.

The following is a list of some of the more popular general-purpose gamification platform vendors:

• Bunchball (bunchball.com)—Founded in 2005, Bunchball provides the Nitro gamification platform, as well as some integrated solutions and APIs for a number of enterprise solutions.

• Badgeville (badgeville.com)—Founded in 2010, Badgeville offers the Behavior Platform for gamification, as well as some integrated solutions and APIs for enterprise solutions.

- BigDoor (bigdoor.com)—Founded in 2009, BigDoor provides a gamification platform that focuses primarily on consumer-facing solutions.

Given the fast-changing nature of gamification vendor services, remember to seek out current information and status regarding these and other vendors. The examples used in this section are intended to be just that—examples. These do not represent complete lists, nor should they be considered any type of endorsement.

PROMOTING AND LAUNCHING

In the movie *Field of Dreams*, Kevin Costner plays an Iowa corn farmer (Ray Kinsella) who hears a voice telling him, "If you build it, he will come."[1] Ray interprets the message to mean that if he builds a baseball field, the ghosts of Shoeless Joe Jackson and the Chicago White Sox will come to play. Ray builds the field, and Shoeless Joe and the White Sox do come, as well as many people who come to watch the baseball game. He built it, and they came. It's great that in the movies you can dream "if you build it, they will come," and your dream might just come true. Real life doesn't work that way.

Organizations often underestimate the promotion effort required to attract and engage the target audience. In some cases, the solution will be promoted to the public at large, as we saw with Quirky and Khan Academy. In other cases, there will be a bounded audience of employees, customers, or a previously established community of interest. Regardless of whether you have preexisting relationships with the target audience, players will need to be encouraged to participate.

As we have already established, even if you have a captive audience for your solution, it is best to encourage the players to opt in to engage with the solution rather than requiring mandatory participation. You will need to promote the gamified solution to drive participation. You should start planning how you will market your solution right from the beginning. If you have a marketing team within your organization, they should form part of the project team from the start. If you aren't lucky enough to have an internal marketing team at your disposal, you can engage an external marketing partner.

A marketing plan must be developed that focuses on the activities to promote the solution. The nature of the plan will depend largely on the target audience and the nature of any pre-existing relationship with them. Externally focused solutions will typically leverage nontraditional channels such as social media presence, YouTube videos, Google and Facebook advertisements, blogs, and other channels. In any case, you need to build awareness in the target audience as a first step in getting people to engage with the solution. Internally focused solutions will require a marketing plan that leverages the internal social media, e-mail, or other more creative approaches.

The team at DWP, described in chapter 5, discovered that they had underestimated the effort required to attract players to Idea Street. Planting the seeds of interest through effective marketing of Idea Street was key in developing that critical mass of participants that enabled it to ultimately go viral. The innovation team tackled this challenge head on with all the usual marketing strategies, but also went beyond. The team developed interest by sitting in the foyers of DWP buildings and signing people up directly—and even handing out "DWPeas" (the kind people eat) to potential participants to spark interest.

Because of the social nature of many gamified solutions, it is important to achieve critical mass before the solution can become really effective. The players of the game can become its best advocates. One of the things Zynga does really well (or annoyingly well) is to leverage Facebook to spread the word about their games. Posting accomplishments that are exposed to friends on Facebook is a great way to make your message go viral.

Creating awareness, building the user base, and achieving critical mass are important steps in successfully launching a gamified solution. Plan the promotion of the solution and invest in building the user base from the outset of the project.

MANAGING THE BENEFITS

Benefits realization starts at the beginning of the project with the definition of the target business outcomes. Once the project is initiated, it must constantly align with the business outcomes that are being addressed. Early in the project, a measurement system must be identified or established to baseline the measures that will be used. The baseline enables you to determine if the project was successful in achieving the target business outcomes that were defined at the beginning of the project. Once the project finishes, benefits must be harvested, tracked to schedule, and communicated.

Benefits realization is the responsibility of the project sponsor, the CFO, and the CIO. It focuses on business outcomes that are often broader than simple measures of ROI. Gamification projects tend to focus on areas that have a causal relationship to revenue, costs, and profits. The leading indicators such as driving website traffic, increasing learning retention, and launching innovation projects predict downstream business results. Project teams should understand and communicate the causal relationships between the leading indicators that the project is focused on and the follow-on business performance impacts.

Quite often, gamification projects result in unanticipated benefits. For example, an innovation management solution may have the unanticipated benefit of improving communication across business areas, or a customer-facing solution to encourage brand advocacy may also result in customers providing product support. During the benefit harvesting cycle, project team members should watch out for unanticipated benefits and record these as well.

Communicating project success fulfills the promise and closes the loop for project participants. Project successes should be broadly communicated, and not just in terms of the business outcomes that were achieved. Often, anecdotal evidence can have a deeper impact on people's perceptions of project success—these stories make the project come to life. Solicit feedback from players to understand how the solution is helping them achieve their goals, and communicate these stories back to project stakeholders.

No project goes exactly as planned. Inevitably, there will be some setbacks that could have been avoided. The value in these setbacks is to learn from them so other projects can avoid repeating them. Understanding, documenting, and communicating the "lessons learned" is valuable for future projects, and it is also a clear indicator of change management maturity. Along with communicating the benefits achieved, project teams should also communicate the lessons learned.

WRAP UP

✓ If you are attempting to initiate a gamification project, you may need to dispel some common myths and sell the concept of gamification before management will even consider investing in it.

✓ Collect case studies of successes in other organizations to convince management that those successes can be replicated in your company.

✓ A gamification project is unlike most other IT projects, and it requires many different skills to be successful.

✓ Because gamification projects tend to be smaller than other change projects in an organization, sometimes they are not taken seriously and suffer from "hobby project" status.

✓ Assess which approach your organization will use to develop a gamification solution: custom development, purpose-built solutions, or generalized gamification platforms.

✓ The greatest risk in gamification is poorly designed solutions, and the largest barrier to success is the lack of gamification design skills within organizations.

✓ Don't expect that "if you build it, they will come." Plan to invest time and money to market the gamified solution through the launch to develop a critical mass of players.

✓ Benefits realization starts at the beginning of the project and must be tracked, harvested, and communicated.

✓ Watch out for unanticipated benefits and record those as well.

✓ Capture lessons learned to build the organizational memory.

10

Gamification 2020: What the Future Holds

Some organizations today are skeptical about the viability and longevity of gamification as a means to engage and motivate target audiences, and people struggle to understand the trend and its longer-term implications. In a 2012 survey conducted by Pew Research Center, 53 percent of people surveyed said that by 2020 the use of gamification will be widespread, while 42 percent predicted that by 2020 gamification will not evolve to be a larger trend except in specific realms.[1]

In the introduction to this book, we saw that in the 2013 Hype Cycle for Emerging Technologies, Gartner places gamification near the "peak of inflated expectations," and it is heading into the "trough of disillusionment." We expect that gamification will enter the trough of disillusionment in 2014, driven primarily by a lack of understanding of experience design and player engagement strategies, resulting in many failed applications. But we also believe that gamification, applied with correct design principles, will have a significant impact in many domains, and in some fields the use of gamification will be transformational.

In this chapter, we will explore some scenarios for gamification in the 2020 time frame. Bright spots such as Khan Academy, Quirky, and Nike+ prove that gamification can be successfully used to motivate people to achieve their goals. They are exemplars of the three broad areas where gamification is most successfully used: developing skills, driving innovation, and changing behaviors.

Gartner refers to cloud, mobility, social, and information as the nexus of forces that are driving transformational change, and each of these has played a huge part in the rise of gamification to date. Foursquare, the original standard-bearer for gamification, leveraged all of these trends and technologies. In fact, Foursquare was only possible because of the broad acceptance of smartphones outfitted with GPS technologies, and like many smartphone applications, the bulk of the computing in Foursquare is done in the cloud. The viral adoption of Foursquare was to a great extent enabled by the integration with social media tools like Facebook. Foursquare was able to capture location-based information to make context-specific offers to its users in a way that was never before possible.

In the year 2020, people will look at the world quite differently, thanks to technologies that are emerging today. Computers will not only know where you are, they will see what you are doing, sense your mood, learn your habits, understand your needs, and provide you with the information you need, whenever and wherever you need it. There will be a fundamental shift in the way we interact with technology. Instead of being a passive tool, it will become an essential partner that anticipates your needs and provides for them. The role of your smartphone becomes reversed, shifting from a pull model to a push model of information delivery. For example, instead of *you* figuring out that you need to get across the city for an appointment, in the future your smartphone will be checking your schedule, and, knowing where you have to be, it will check the traffic conditions, calculate the time you need to get there, and call the taxi for you. Perhaps surprisingly, your smartphone will direct a large part of your life.

FUTURE SCENARIOS

Gamification will continue to evolve and create new discontinuities in the future. While gamification will not be solely responsible for these changes, it will provide the tools for player interaction and the motivation layer to drive engagement. There are a number of contributing trends that will enable these discontinuities. When thinking about gamification in the year 2020, we need to think of it in the context of how we will interact with technology at that time. The maturation of other emerging technologies, including gesture control, emotion detection, head-mounted displays, and augmented reality will further gamification in many domains by seamlessly integrating technology into our daily lives. Other trends like participatory government, massive open online courses (MOOCs), crowdsourcing, and microcredentials will also play a role in the evolution of gamification.

Combined, these trends will fundamentally change the way we think about learning, problem solving, and personal development. New models will evolve that will become a threat to the status quo for traditional educators, public policy developers, and personal coaches of all kinds. Let's take a look at some scenarios for gamification in 2020 in each of the three application areas: developing skills, driving innovation, and changing behaviors.

THE DEMOCRATIZATION OF LEARNING

Access to advanced education, particularly for people in developing countries, is prohibitively expensive and available only to the elite. A university degree remains the badge of choice for entry into the workforce, but things are changing. Employers are less interested in where you are from or the university you attended than they are in the skills you bring to the table. There are many ways to learn, and gamification, along with other trends in education, is changing the way that people think about learning, advanced education, and recognition of skills attainment.

Engaging students in learning. As we have seen, gamification has been applied to training and education in many different ways to increase the engagement of students in the learning process. In its simplest form, gamification is being applied as a game layer to course material to accelerate feedback loops and provide social recognition rewards that increase student/player engagement in learning, resulting in better learning outcomes. More sophisticated gamification design approaches will develop over time.

Access to advanced education. MOOCs and educational resources such as Khan Academy are changing the face of education. Over the past couple of years, a large number of courses offered by universities have become available online and free for anyone who has an interest in signing up. For example, Coursera currently offers more than five hundred courses from more than one hundred universities and partners, and has signed up more than five million students. Class sizes are huge, often in the tens of thousands, but the time commitment for professors is minimized through on-demand video lectures, online tests, and peer review of work assignments.

Most courses taken through free online delivery services do not provide course credits. However, that is evolving. Some of the courses on Coursera are now included in the Signature Track, which (for a fee) provides verified certificates of course completion. The result is that quality courses are available to anyone who has a computer and an Internet connection, regardless of where they are or their economic means.

Recognition of skills attainment. A key component of education is the broad recognition of the skills that have been attained. Skills may be attained through higher education, work experience, or independent study, but higher education institutions have a virtual stranglehold on recognition of knowledge attainment, and usually only provide that recognition (in the form of a degree) to students who have paid their fees and attended the classes. That may soon change.

As we have discussed previously, certified badges such as those provided through the Mozilla Open Badges project and Coursera's Signature Track provide institutions and learners with a portable electronic means of showcasing achievements. Open badges can be issued by any organization, and the issuance and criteria can be verified with the issuing organization. These badges are relatively new but have seen rapid uptake by institutions. The advantage of open badges is that it provides an infrastructure for verification of accomplishments on a common platform. The value of an open badge will be based on the credibility of the issuing organization and the criteria for achievement. Of course, the value of an achievement is determined by potential employers, not by the issuers.

In the near term, gamification will be used primarily to create more engaging course material. But by 2020, advanced education will be global, with increased equality of access to education and more open recognition of skill attainment through badges. Alternatives to formal higher education can evolve to make education more engaging, widely accessible, and broadly recognized. Learners will not be inhibited by geography or socioeconomic status. Employers will have a broader choice of skilled candidates. Countries that have traditionally suffered from shortages of highly skilled labor will have access to a new local talent pool. The impact will be significant for educational institutions, organizations, and developing economies.

TACKLING WICKED PROBLEMS WITH
STAKEHOLDER POWER

As we have already seen, gamification and innovation make a great couple. Barclaycard, Quirky, and DWP demonstrate the power of collaborative idea development. These types of innovation solutions will continue to grow, but in the future gamified solutions will also start to take on really hard problems.

The term "wicked problem" was first used by Horst Rittel and Melvin Webber to describe a class of problem that could not be tackled by scientific approaches. They described public policy problems as "wicked," in contrast to scientific problems, which are "tame." In their analysis they wrote:

> Policy problems cannot be definitively described. Moreover, in a pluralistic society there is nothing like the undisputable public good; there is no objective definition of equity; policies that respond to social problems cannot be meaningfully correct or false; and it makes no sense to talk about "optimal solutions" to social problems unless severe qualifications are imposed first. Even worse, there are no "solutions: in the sense of definitive and objective answers."[2]

Wicked problems most often occur in the social context and can be influenced by public policy. Global examples include climate change, sustainability, drug trafficking, and financial regulation. Local examples include problems like highway expansions, school closures, and waste landfill placement. These problems should be addressed by public policy, but the challenge is to find a path forward. Inevitably, these problems have stakeholders with different points of view and vested interests in the outcome, and there is not a single solution that will satisfy all the stakeholders' interests.

Tame problems have a solution, wicked problems do not. Tame problems are like puzzles, wicked problems are like games. According to the Supreme Court of India, the difference between a puzzle and a game is that in a puzzle the outcome is predetermined, and in a game it is not.[3] Scientific approaches can solve really tough puzzles, but to solve wicked problems, we need to create gamified emergent solutions.

Because most wicked problems fall within the realm of public policy, politics is the principal barrier in moving forward. Public policy development may include input from government experts, interest groups, and citizens. The policy itself is crafted by policy developers within government. These teams try to balance out the costs and trade-offs to create a policy proposal, often in the form of new legislation, that will be voted on by elected officials. Politicians are reluctant to make any move that will disenfranchise a large part of the electorate, and since by definition wicked problems do not have an optimal solution, like deer in the headlights, politicians hesitate to make any move at all.

Because public policy is inevitably drafted by a closed circle within a government policy development team, stakeholders do not always feel that their interests are appropriately represented. It is the kind of ivory tower problem that we discussed earlier, where innovation is highly centralized with a group of big brains that are often disconnected from the stakeholders and the problem to be addressed. Stakeholders feel disenfranchised, as they did not play a direct role in policy development.

Another way is possible. Recently, governments have been devolving some of the decision-making power to the people they represent. The moves are small, but they are starting. For example:

- A number of communities, such as Harford County in Maryland[4] and the city of San Francisco,[5] are using gamified solutions to engage citizens and capture ideas for community improvement projects.

- Some communities are implementing participatory budgeting for at least a part of their overall budget. What this means is that the community identifies project priorities and the priorities are developed into spending proposals, which are voted on by the community. The process was first put into place in Porto Alegre in Brazil, and has been adopted by many other municipalities around the world.

- Finland has implemented a Citizens Initiative Act, which allows ordinary citizens to propose laws if they can gather fifty thousand signatures for the proposal. The Open Ministry in Finland is a nonprofit organization that works with citizen groups to develop legislation under the Citizens Initiative. The Open Ministry uses various development processes, but recently crowdsourced a proposal for reforming copyright laws in Finland.[6]

There are many other initiatives in participatory democracy, and it is moving in the right direction, but more can be done. Governments still maintain full control over citizen participation. Public servants need to recognize that it's not *their* government. The role of government must be to facilitate the development of public policy by the stakeholders and citizens. This is where gamification can play a role in addressing wicked problems.

Rather than having government design policy solutions for wicked problems, it needs to design gamified solutions that will enable policy development by the stakeholders and citizens. Only then will collaborative solutions for wicked problems emerge with the broad support of stakeholders and citizens, thus ensuring that public support is in place for politicians to risk supporting legislative change.

YOUR SMARTPHONE BECOMES YOUR PERSONAL COACH

Currently, dozens of gamified applications exist to modify personal behaviors, but they are relatively unsophisticated and are often little more than reminder systems with some points and badges slapped on. More effective systems integrate with social networks to reinforce motivation with social recognition. Examples include gamified applications to coach people to lose weight, quit smoking, improve fitness, correct posture, manage personal finances, take medication, and improve memory.

While gamification design will continually improve to provide the motivation for personal development, by 2020 adoption of personal development applications will increase significantly, driven by the maturation of emerging technologies such as head-mounted displays, augmented reality, natural-language interfaces, gesture control, and emotion detection. All of these technologies will enable gamified personal development applications to talk to you, see what you are doing, know how you are feeling, and adjust based on your condition. You will no longer have to take out your smartphone and open an application. Your personal assistant will simply be there when you need it. Imagine a supersmart and sensitive Siri.

Gesture control. This enables free-air gesture recognition, allowing the user to control devices without actually touching anything. With gesture control, a computer can "see" what you are doing. The most common and accessible device for gesture control today is the Microsoft Kinect controller, which is already being used in some gamification solutions for rehabilitation and fitness training. The technology is already available at reasonable price points and will advance in sophistication over the next few years.

Emotion detection. In the future, your computer will not only see what you are doing, it will also sense how you are feeling. Emotion detection today is most developed in voice analysis and it is primarily used in call centers to detect angry callers. But the technology is advancing to also include facial expression analysis and body movements. Once computers are able to determine if you are angry, stressed, happy, or depressed, they will be able to quickly adapt to your current mood.

Head-mounted displays. The technology has been around for a while, primarily used in military applications. For example, pilots have a display built into their helmet that provides information in addition to what they see through the visor (augmented reality). Google Glass will be the first broadly available head-mounted display that is targeted at the consumer market. By 2020, the technology will become less intrusive, moving to heads-up displays in which the display is either integrated into or paired with contact lenses. In all cases, the user perceives the virtual image at an ideal viewing distance, although no screen is present.

Augmented reality. Augmented reality provides a bridge between the digital and physical worlds. It adds context-relevant information to real-world scenes using text and graphics. In consumer applications today, augmented reality is most often delivered on smartphones, where the camera displays scenes in real time and information is augmented from other sources. Currently, the technology is most often used in specialized applications, often in conjunction with head-mounted displays, such as in the military example described above. As consumer head-mounted display technologies evolve, augmented reality technologies will follow.

Incorporating expert advice into gamified personal coaching systems along with these technologies will enable a richer coaching experience. For example, a simple gamified personal development system like the ones available today can tell you to do twenty push-ups and award you points for completing them—because that's what it's programmed to do. With the incorporation of these emerging technologies and expert advice in the future, a gamified personal fitness coach can tell you to do push-ups, evaluate and correct your posture while you are doing those push-ups, assess your exertion, adjust the number of push-ups to match your level of fitness, and encourage you every step of the way. This richer personal coaching experience will be compelling for many applications.

Health care, governments, and other organizations that promote healthier lifestyles, improved personal finance, or other improvement in lifestyle change can benefit from the use of gamification to more deeply engage the target audience without the costs of hiring human coaches. These organizations must specifically identify the required behavior change and the target audience, and begin to leverage gamification in applications that address these behavior changes.

CONCLUSION: RETHINKING MOTIVATION IN A CONNECTED WORLD

Nobody wins the human race. The only way to win at life is to set your own course, to work hard to achieve your goals, and to contribute to something that is bigger than yourself. We don't win this race individually, we all win together. People who are inspired can do these things, no matter what course they choose.

People haven't changed. We have always been motivated by the same things. What has changed is the world we live in, and how we interact with it. We are no longer surrounded by just our family, friends, and community. We are now connected in real time to all kinds of communities through technology. Our connections have shifted from the purely physical to the digital, eliminating barriers of scale, time, and distance.

Gamification is not new. Game mechanics and design have been used to engage and motivate people to achieve their goals throughout recorded history. Gamification is about rethinking motivation in a world where we are more often connected digitally than physically. It is about building motivation into a digitally engaged world. And we are just getting started in this journey. Gamification will continue to develop for many years to come.

My hope is that *Gamify* has given you a new way to think about motivation, and that together we can help people live happier and more fulfilled lives by motivating them to achieve their goals.

NOTES

Introduction

1 Kathleen Lessman, e-mail to author, January 17, 2013.
2 "About Foursquare," Foursquare, accessed November 18, 2013, https://foursquare.com/about.
3 Google Trends, Google, accessed December 4, 2013, http://www.google.com/trends/explore#q=gamification
4 Nick Pelling, "The (Short) Prehistory of "Gamification," *Funding Startups (& Other Impossibilities)* blog, August 9, 2011, accessed November 18, 2013, http://nanodome.wordpress.com/2011/08/09/the-short-prehistory-of-gamification/.
5 "SQUEEZED MIDDLE is named Oxford Dictionaries Word of the Year 2011," Oxford University Press via PR Newswire, November 22, 2011, accessed November 18, 2013, http://www.prnewswire.com/news-releases-test/squeezed-middle-is-named-oxford-dictionaries-word-of-the-year-2011-134361588.html.
6 Jackie Fenn and Mark Raskino, "Understanding Gartner's Hype Cycles," Gartner, July 2, 2013, http://www.gartner.com/document/code/251964.

Chapter 1

1 Kevin Kruse, "Why Employee Engagement? (These 28 Research Studies Prove the Benefits)," *Forbes*, September 4, 2012, accessed November 18, 2013, http://www.forbes.com/sites/kevinkruse/2012/09/04/why-employee-engagement.
2 Nikki Blacksmith and Jim Harter, "Majority of American Workers Not Engaged in Their Jobs," Gallup, October 28, 2011, accessed November 18, 2013, http://www.gallup.com/poll/150383/Majority-American-Workers-Not-Engaged-Jobs.aspx.
3 "New Research Reveals Why Strong Engagement Scores Can Spell Trouble for Organisations," Chartered Institute of Personnel and Development, May 23, 2012, accessed November 18, 2013, http://

www.cipd.co.uk/pressoffice/press-releases/Strong-engagement-scores
-can-spell-trouble-for-organisations-230512.aspx.

4 Dr. Jennifer Stinson, telephone interview with author, June 28, 2013.

5 Stuart Thom and Cory Eisentraut, telephone interview with author, June 26, 2013.

6 "Pain Squad Mobile App," Cundari video, 2:35, accessed November 18, 2013, http://www.campaignpage.ca/sickkidsapp/.

7 Daniel Pink, *Drive: The Surprising Truth About What Motivates Us* (New York: Riverhead Books, 2009) Kindle edition, Chapter: Introduction, loc. 183.

8 MasterCard, accessed December 4, 2013, http://www.mastercard.us/ads-and-offers.html

Chapter 2

1 *Up in the Air,* directed by Jason Reitman, 2009, Paramount Pictures.

2 Ian Bogost, "Gamification Is Bullshit," *The Atlantic*, August 9, 2011, accessed November 18, 2013, http://www.theatlantic.com/technology/archive/2011/08/gamification-is-bullshit/243338/.

3 Jesse Schell, *2013 D.I.C.E Summit*, video 4:55, accessed November 19, 2013, http://www.dicesummit.org/video_gallery/video_gallery_2013.asp.

4 Backgrounder, Free The Children, page 2, accessed December 4, 2013, http://cdn6.freethechildren.com/wp-content/uploads/2013/09/FTC-PR-backgrounder-V4.pdf

5 Craig Kielburger, Telephone interview with author, October 31, 2013.

6 "Weight Watchers Announces Second Quarter 2013 Results and Revises Its Fiscal 2013 Guidance," Weight Watchers, August 1, 2013, accessed November 19, 2013, http://www.weightwatchersinternational.com/phoenix.zhtml?c=130178&p=irol-newsArticle&ID=1843897&highlight=.

7 Nicholas P. Hotchkin, "Weight Watchers International Management Discusses Q2 2013 Results—Earnings Call Transcript," Seeking Alpha, accessed November 19, 2013, http://seekingalpha.com/article/1597092-weight-watchers-international-management-discusses-q2-2013-results-earnings-call-transcript?page=6.

Chapter 3

1 Geoffrey Bachelor Hill Jr., Facebook message to author, July 8, 2012.

2 "About Nike, Inc.," Nike, accessed November 19, 2013, http://nikeinc.com/pages/about-nike-inc.

3 Stefan Olander, "Running Nike's Digital Strategy," WIRED Business Conference 2012, video 16:05, accessed November 19, 2013, http://fora.tv/2012/05/01/WIRED_Business_Conference_Testing_Your_Limits.

4 Sam Laird, "Nike+ Users Could Power 6,700 Houses Daily," February 23, 2013, accessed November 19, 2013, http://mashable.com/2013/02/22/nike-fuelband-stats/.

5 Rod Morris, telephone interview with author, July 30, 2013.

6 "Company," Opower, accessed November 19, 2013, http://www.opower.com/company.

7 Darren Jacoby and Spencer Reiss, "Vail Resorts Creates Epic Experiences with Customer Intelligence," SAS Institute, accessed November 19, 2013, http://www.sas.com/reg/gen/corp/1908549-customer-analytics.

8 E.B. Boyd, "Baked In: Vail Resorts' EpicMix Scores Customer Loyalty by Tracking Slope Skills," *Fast Company*, April 21, 2011, accessed November 19, 2013. http://www.fastcompany.com/1748940/baked-vail-resorts-epicmix-scores-customer-loyalty-tracking-slope-skills

9 Kathleen Lessman, e-mail to author, January 17, 2013.

10 Brian Burke, "Migrating Customers to Online Services Using Gamification," Gartner, March 1, 2013.

11 Kelly Liyakasa, "Game On: Gamification Strategies Motivate Customer and Employee Behaviors," Destination CRM, May 2012, Accessed December 4, 2013, http://www.destinationcrm.com/Articles/Editorial/Magazine-Features/Game-On-Gamification-Strategies-Motivate-Customer-and-Employee-Behaviors-81866.aspx.

12 Sven Gerjets and Russell Bacon, telephone interview with author, November 18, 2013.

13 Imran Sayeed and Naureen Meraj, telephone interview with author, January 12, 2013.

14 Tom Austin, "Predicts 2013: Social and Collaboration Go Deeper and Wider," Gartner, November 28, 2012, http://www.gartner.com/document/2254316.

15 Dr. John Kotter, "The 8-Step Process for Leading Change," Kotter International, accessed November 19, 2013, http://www.kotterinternational.com/our-principles/changesteps.

16 Brian Burke, "Motivating Healthy Choices With Gamification," Gartner, April 10, 2013.

17 "Daily Challenge", MeYou Health, accessed December 4, 2013, http://meyouhealth.com/daily-challenge/.

18 "Friends/Find Friends/Facebook," Nike+, accessed November 19, 2013, https://secure-nikeplus.nike.com/plus/friends/UserName/#facebook.

Chapter 4

1 Tanis, letter to Salman Khan, Khan Academy, December 15, 2012, accessed November 19, 2013, https://www.khanacademy.org/stories/tanis-december-15-2012.

2 "Fact Sheet," Khan Academy, November 1, 2013, accessed November 19, 2013, https://dl.dropboxusercontent.com/u/33330500/KAFactSheet .zip.

3 "About Badging," Center for Educational Technologies, accessed November 19, 2013, http://badges.cet.edu/about.html.

4 "NASA Lunar Rover Geometry Badge," Center for Educational Technologies, accessed November 19, 2013, http://badges.cet.edu/Lunar Rover/.

5 "Privacy & Security Training Games," Health IT, accessed November 19, 2013, http://www.healthit.gov/providers-professionals/privacy -security-training-games.

6 "About," Duolingo, accessed November 19, 2013, http://www.duol ingo.com/info.

7 Wall Street Survivor, http://www.wallstreetsurvivor.com.

8 Imran Sayeed and Naureen Meraj, NTT Data telephone interview with author, October 17, 2013.

9 "Consumers Don't Understand Health Insurance, Carnegie Mellon Research Shows," Carnegie Mellon University, August 1, 2013, accessed November 19, 2013, http://www.cmu.edu/news/stories/archives/2013/august/aug1_understandinghealthinsurance.html.

10 "Health Insurance Marketplaces," Capital Blue Cross, accessed November 19, 2013, https://capbluecross.healthcareu.com/en.

11 Clayton Nicholas, telephone interview with author, October 30, 2013.

12 "Case Study: Autodesk," Badgeville, accessed November 19, 2013, http://badgeville.com/customer/case-study/autodesk.

Chapter 5

1 Brian Burke, "Case Study: Innovation Squared: The Department for Work and Pensions Turns Innovation Into a Game," Gartner, November 23, 2010.

2 Duncan Mcgugan, e-mail to author, January 9, 2013.

3 "About," Quirky, accessed November 16, 2013, http://www.quirky
.com/about.
4 Paul Wilmore, interview with author, October 30, 2013.

Chapter 6

1 "About IDEO," IDEO, accessed November 19, 2013, http://www
.ideo.com/about/.

Chapter 8

1 Natasha Mohanty, "Shareable Google News Badges for Your Favorite Topics," *Google News Blog*, July 14, 2011, accessed November
19, 2013, http://googlenewsblog.blogspot.com.es/2011/07/shareable
-google-news-badges-for-your.html.
2 Yossi Matias, "More Spring Cleaning," *Google Official Blog*, September 28, 2012, accessed November 19, 2013, http://googleblog
.blogspot.com.es/2012/09/more-spring-cleaning.html.
3 "Welcome to the DARPA Robotics Challenge Website," DARPA,
accessed November 19, 2013, http://www.theroboticschallenge.org/.
4 Mihály Csíkszentmihályi, *Flow: The Psychology of Optimal Experience*
(New York: Harper & Rowe, 1990).
5 Ethan Mollick and Nancy Rothbard, "Mandatory Fun: Gamification and the Impact of Games at Work" (Management Department,
The Wharton School, University of Pennsylvania, June 5, 2013), 32,
http://papers.ssrn.com/sol3/papers.cfm?abstract_id=2277103.
6 KoolAidGuy, "Why Digg's Non-Hierarchical Editorial Control Does
Not Work and How to Exploit It," December 13, 2005, accessed
November 19, 2013, http://koolaidguy.blogspot.com.es/.
7 Richard MacManus, "Gaming Digg: The KoolAidGuy Saga," ZDNet,
December 27, 2005, accessed November 19, 2013, http://www.zdnet
.com/blog/web2explorer/gaming-digg-the-koolaidguy-saga/90.

Chapter 9

1 *Field of Dreams*, directed by Phil Alden Robinson, 1989, Universal
Studios Entertainment.

Chapter 10

1 Janna Quitney Anderson and Lee Rainie, "Gamification: Experts
Expect 'Game Layers' to Expand in the Future, with Positive and

Negative Results," Pew Research Center, May 18, 2012, accessed November 19, 2013, http://pewinternet.org/Reports/2012/Future-of -Gamification.aspx.

2 With kind permission from Springer Science+Business Media: Policy Sciences, "Dilemmas in a general theory of planning", volume 4, issue 2, June 1973, page 155, Horst W. J. Rittel, Melvin M. Webber.

3 S H Kapadia, "M/S Pleasantime Products Etc. vs Commr. of Central Excise," Supreme Court of India, November 12, 2009, accessed November 19, 2013, http://www.indiankanoon.org/doc/620872/.

4 "Harford County Leverages Spigit to Capture Cost-Saving Ideas," Spigit, accessed November 19, 2013, http://www.spigit.com/media -center/case-studies/#prettyPhoto.

5 "City of San Francisco, Cost Savings and Revenue Generation," Brightidea, accessed November 19, 2013, http://www.brightidea .com/customers-government.bix.

6 "What Are the Finns Up To?" *Reimagining Democracy*, August 21, 2013, accessed November 13, 2013, http://democracyoneday .com/2013/08/21/what-are-the-finns-up-to/.

REFERENCES

Alden Robinson, Phil. *Field of Dreams*. Universal Studios Entertainment, 1989.

Austin, Tom. "Predicts 2013: Social and Collaboration Go Deeper and Wider." Gartner. November 28, 2012. http://www.gartner.com/doc ument/2254316.

Bachelor Hill Jr., Geoffrey. Facebook message to author. July 8, 2012.

Badgeville. "Case Study: Autodesk." Accessed November 19, 2013. http://badgeville.com/customer/case-study/autodesk.

Blacksmith, Nikki and Jim Harter. "Majority of American Workers Not Engaged in Their Jobs." Gallup. October 28, 2011. Accessed November 18, 2013. http://www.gallup.com/poll/150383/Majority-American -Workers-Not-Engaged-Jobs.aspx.

Bogost, Ian. "Gamification Is Bullshit." *The Atlantic*. August 9, 2011. Accessed November 18, 2013, http://www.theatlantic.com/technol ogy/archive/2011/08/gamification-is-bullshit/243338/.

Boyd, E.B. "Baked In: Vail Resorts' EpicMix Scores Customer Loyalty by Tracking Slope Skills." *Fast Company*. April 21, 2011. Accessed November 19, 2013. http://www.fastcompany.com/1748940/baked -vail-resorts-epicmix-scores-customer-loyalty-tracking-slope-skills.

Brightidea. "City of San Francisco, Cost Savings and Revenue Genera-tion." Accessed November 19, 2013. http://www.brightidea.com/ customers-government.bix.

Burke, Brian. "Case Study: Innovation Squared: The Department for Work and Pensions Turns Innovation Into a Game." Gartner. November 23, 2010.

Burke, Brian. "Migrating Customers to Online Services Using Gamifica-tion." Gartner. March 1, 2013.

Burke, Brian. "Motivating Healthy Choices With Gamification." Gart-ner. April 10, 2013.

Capital Blue Cross. "Health Insurance Marketplaces." Accessed November 19, 2013. https://capbluecross.healthcareu.com/en.

Carnegie Mellon University. "Consumers Don't Understand Health Insurance, Carnegie Mellon Research Shows." August 1, 2013. Accessed November 19, 2013. http://www.cmu.edu/news/stories/archives/2013/august/aug1_understandinghealthinsurance.html.

Center for Educational Technologies. "About Badging." Accessed November 19, 2013. http://badges.cet.edu/about.html.

Center for Educational Technologies. "NASA Lunar Rover Geometry Badge." Accessed November 19, 2013. http://badges.cet.edu/Lunar Rover/.

Chartered Institute of Personnel and Development. "New Research Reveals Why Strong Engagement Scores Can Spell Trouble for Organisations." May 23, 2012. Accessed November 18, 2013. http://www.cipd.co.uk/pressoffice/press-releases/Strong-engagement-scores-can-spell-trouble-for-organisations-230512.aspx.

Csíkszentmihályi, Mihály. *Flow: The Psychology of Optimal Experience* (New York: Harper & Row, 1990).

Cundari. "Pain Squad Mobile App." Video, 2:35. Accessed November 18, 2013. http://www.campaignpage.ca/sickkidsapp/.

DARPA. "Welcome to the DARPA Robotics Challenge Website." Accessed November 19, 2013. http://www.theroboticschallenge.org/.

Duolingo. "About." Accessed November 19, 2013. http://www.duolingo.com/info.

Fenn, Jackie and Mark Raskino. "Understanding Gartner's Hype Cycles." Gartner. July 2, 2013. http://www.gartner.com/document/code/251964.

Foursquare. "About Foursquare." Accessed November 18, 2013. https://foursquare.com/about.

Free the Children. Backgrounder. Accessed December 4, 2013. http://cdn6.freethechildren.com/wp-content/uploads/2013/09/FTC-PR-backgrounder-V4.pdf

Gerjets, Sven and Russell Bacon. Telephone interview with author. November 18, 2013.

Google. "Google Trends." Accessed December 4, 2013. http://www.google.com/trends/explore#q=gamification.

Health IT. "Privacy & Security Training Games." Accessed November 19, 2013. http://www.healthit.gov/providers-professionals/privacy-security-training-games.

Hotchkin, Nicholas P. "Weight Watchers International Management Discusses Q2 2013 Results—Earnings Call Transcript." Seeking Alpha.

Accessed November 19, 2013. http://seekingalpha.com/article/1597092
-weight-watchers-international-management-discusses-q2-2013-results
-earnings-call-transcript?page=6.

IDEO. "About IDEO." Accessed November 19, 2013. http://www.ideo
.com/about/.

Jacoby, Darren and Spencer Reiss. "Vail Resorts Creates Epic Experiences with Customer Intelligence." SAS Institute. Accessed November
19, 2013. http://www.sas.com/reg/gen/corp/1908549-customer-ana
lytics.

Kapadia, S H. "M/S Pleasantime Products Etc. vs Commr. of Central
Excise." Supreme Court of India. November 12, 2009. Accessed
November 19, 2013. http://www.indiankanoon.org/doc/620872/.

Khan Academy. "Fact Sheet." November 1, 2013. Accessed November
19, 2013. https://dl.dropboxusercontent.com/u/33330500/KAFact
Sheet.zip.

Kielburger, Craig. Telephone interview with author. October 31, 2013.

KoolAidGuy. "Why Digg's Non-Hierarchical Editorial Control Does
Not Work and How to Exploit It." December 13, 2005. Accessed
November 19, 2013. http://koolaidguy.blogspot.com.es/.

Kotter, Dr. John. "The 8-Step Process for Leading Change." Kotter International. Accessed November 19, 2013. http://www.kotterinternational
.com/our-principles/changesteps.

Kruse, Kevin. "Why Employee Engagement? (These 28 Research Studies
Prove the Benefits)." *Forbes*. September 4, 2012. Accessed November
18, 2013. http://www.forbes.com/sites/kevinkruse/2012/09/04/why
-employee-engagement.

Laird, Sam. "Nike+ Users Could Power 6,700 Houses Daily." *Mashable*.
February 23, 2013. Accessed November 19, 2013. http://mashable
.com/2013/02/22/nike-fuelband-stats/.

Lessman, Kathleen. E-Mail to author. January 17, 2013.

Liyakasa, Kelly. "Game On: Gamification Strategies Motivate Customer
and Employee Behaviors." Destination CRM. May 2012. Accessed
December 4, 2013. http://www.destinationcrm.com/Articles/Edito
rial/Magazine-Features/Game-On-Gamification-Strategies-Moti
vate-Customer-and-Employee-Behaviors-81866.aspx

MacManus, Richard. "Gaming Digg: The KoolAidGuy Saga." ZDNet.
December 27, 2005. Accessed November 19, 2013. http://www.zdnet
.com/blog/web2explorer/gaming-digg-the-koolaidguy-saga/90.

MasterCard. Accessed December 4, 2013. http://www.mastercard.us/
ads-and-offers.html

Matias, Yossi. "More Spring Cleaning." *Google Official Blog*, September 28, 2012. Accessed November 19, 2013. http://googleblog.blogspot .com.es/2012/09/more-spring-cleaning.html.

Mcgugan, Duncan. E-mail to author. January 9, 2013.

MeYouHealth. "Daily Challenge." Accessed December 4, 2013. http:// meyouhealth.com/daily-challenge/

Mohanty, Natasha. "Shareable Google News Badges for Your Favorite Topics." *Google News Blog*. July 14, 2011. Accessed November 19, 2013.   http://googlenewsblog.blogspot.com.es/2011/07/shareable -google-news-badges-for-your.html.

Mollick, Ethan and Nancy Rothbard. "Mandatory Fun: Gamification and the Impact of Games at Work." Management Department, The Wharton School, University of Pennsylvania. June 5, 2013. http:// papers.ssrn.com/sol3/papers.cfm?abstract_id=2277103.

Morris, Rod. Telephone interview with author. July 30, 2013.

Nicholas, Clayton. Telephone interview with author. October 30, 2013.

Nike. "About Nike, Inc." Accessed November 19, 2013. http://nikeinc .com/pages/about-nike-inc.

Nike+. "Friends/Find Friends/Facebook." Accessed November 19, 2013. https://secure-nikeplus.nike.com/plus/friends/UserName/#facebook.

Olander, Stefan. "Running Nike's Digital Strategy." WIRED Business Conference 2012. Video 16:05. Accessed November 19, 2013. http:// fora.tv/2012/05/01/WIRED_Business_Conference_Testing_Your _Limits.

Olding, Elise. "Gartner's Top Predictions for IT Organizations and Users, 2013 and Beyond: Balancing Economics, Risk, Opportunity and Innovation." Gartner. October 19, 2012.

Opower. "Company." accessed November 19, 2013. http://www.opower .com/company.

Oxford University Press via PR Newswire. "SQUEEZED MIDDLE is named Oxford Dictionaries Word of the Year 2011." November 22, 2011. Accessed November 18, 2013. http://www.prnewswire.com/ news-releases-test/squeezed-middle-is-named-oxford-dictionaries -word-of-the-year-2011-134361588.html.

Pelling, Nick. "The (Short) Prehistory of "Gamification." *Funding Startups (& Other Impossibilities) Blog*. August 9, 2011. Accessed November 18, 2013. http://nanodome.wordpress.com/2011/08/09/ the-short-prehistory-of-gamification/.

Pink, Daniel. *Drive: The Surprising Truth About What Motivates Us*. New York: Riverhead Books, 2009 Kindle edition.

Quirky. "About." Accessed November 16, 2013. http://www.quirky.com/about.

Quitney Anderson, Janna and Lee Rainie, "Gamification: Experts Expect 'Game Layers' to Expand in the Future, with Positive and Negative Results." Pew Research Center. May 18, 2012. Accessed November 19, 2013. http://pewinternet.org/Reports/2012/Future-of-Gamification.aspx.

Re:Imagining Democracy. "What Are the Finns Up To?" August 21, 2013. Accessed November 13, 2013. http://democracyoneday.com/2013/08/21/what-are-the-finns-up-to/.

Reitman, Jason. *Up in the Air*. Paramount Pictures, 2009.

Rittel, Horst W. J. and Melvin M. Webber. *Dilemmas in a General Theory of Planning of Planning*. Elsevier Scientific Publishing Company, 1973. http://www.uctc.net/mwebber/Rittel+Webber+Dilemmas+General_Theory_of_Planning.pdf.

Sayeed, Imran and Naureen Meraj. NTT Data telephone interview with author. October 17, 2013.

Sayeed, Imran and Naureen Meraj. NTT Data telephone interview with author. January 12, 2013.

Schell, Jesse. *2013 D.I.C.E Summit*. Video 4:55. Accessed November 19, 2013. http://www.dicesummit.org/video_gallery/video_gallery_2013.asp.

Spigit. "Harford County Leverages Spigit to Capture Cost-Saving Ideas." Accessed November 19, 2013. http://www.spigit.com/media-center/case-studies/#prettyPhoto.

Stinson, Dr. Jennifer. Telephone interview with author. June 28, 2013.

Tanis. Letter to Salman Khan. Khan Academy. December 15, 2012. Accessed November 19, 2013. https://www.khanacademy.org/stories/tanis-december-15-2012.

Thom, Stuart and Cory Eisentraut. Telephone interview with author. June 26, 2013.

Wall Street Survivor, http://www.wallstreetsurvivor.com.

Weight Watchers. "Weight Watchers Announces Second Quarter 2013 Results and Revises Its Fiscal 2013 Guidance." August 1, 2013. Accessed November 19, 2013. http://www.weightwatchersinternational.com/phoenix.zhtml?c=130178&p=irol-newsArticle&ID=1843897&highlight=.

Wilmore, Paul. Interview with author. October 30, 2013.

INDEX

ABOUT THE AUTHOR

Brian Burke is a vice president at Gartner, covering enterprise architecture for the past fifteen years. Since 2010, he has been leading research on the emerging gamification trend. As an expert in enterprise architecture, he has worked for decades on understanding disruptive technology trends and their implications for business. He currently leads research in business-outcome-driven enterprise architecture, and his groundbreaking work in the development of federated architectures has been implemented in hundreds of organizations in both the public and private sectors. He is also a prominent researcher and speaker in the areas of gamification, enterprise architecture, innovation management and IT strategy. He has been published and interviewed in the *Wall Street Journal*, BBC, USA Today, Financial Times, Inc., The Guardian, and Forbes Online.

Mr. Burke has a broad and diverse background in technology and strategy, having more than 25 years of experience in the industry. He joined Gartner in April 2005 with the acquisition of Meta Group, where he had worked for seven years. Prior to that, he held senior management positions with responsibility for the development of IT strategy and enterprise architecture. He has led many projects implementing emerging technologies.